201 GLUTEN-FREE
RECIPES FOR KIDS

201 GLUTEN-FREE RECIPES FOR KIDS

Chicken Nuggets! Pizza! Birthday Cake! All Your Kids' Favorites—All Gluten-Free!

CARRIE S. FORBES

Adams Media

New York London Toronto Sydney New Delhi

Adams Media
An Imprint of Simon & Schuster, Inc.
57 Littlefield Street
Avon, Massachusetts 02322

For information about special discounts for bulk purchases, please contact Simon & Schuster Special Sales at 1-866-506-1949 or *business@simonandschuster.com*.

The Simon & Schuster Speakers Bureau can bring authors to your live event. For more information or to book an event contact the Simon & Schuster Speakers Bureau at 1-866-248-3049 or visit our website at *www.simonspeakers.com*.

Manufactured in the United States of America

11 2020

Library of Congress Cataloging-in-Publication Data has been applied for.

ISBN 978-1-4405-7083-4
ISBN 978-1-4405-7111-4 (ebook)

Always follow safety and common-sense cooking protocol while using kitchen utensils, operating ovens and stoves, and handling uncooked food. If children are assisting in the preparation of any recipe, they should always be supervised by an adult.

DEDICATION

To owl-loving Madelyn and camo-rocking Kendall, two amazing young girls who taught me how tough and resilient little ones can be in the face of a life-changing celiac diagnosis. Because of that beautiful smile, Madelyn, I've learned how important it is to make sure the parents of young celiac kids have access to a gluten-free support system and a recipe for good ol' gluten-free cinnamon bun muffins.

CONTENTS

CHAPTER 11: **Odds and Ends...207**

APPENDIX: **Online Gluten-Free Resources for Parents...223**

INTRODUCTION

Switching to a gluten-free diet can be difficult. Switching your kids to a gluten-free diet can be even *more* difficult. One way to make the transition easier for them—and you—is by cooking up healthy gluten-free alternatives to their favorite meals. Who's going to miss the gluten when you're making pancakes in the morning, chicken noodle soup for lunch, pizza for dinner, and cupcakes for dessert? With all these options, you won't be switching them over, you'll be winning them over with tasty dishes.

The decision to go gluten-free is one that more and more parents are choosing to make. In some instances, it's because their children suffer from celiac disease or gluten intolerance, and can't have it as part of their diets. In others, it's because they want to treat autism spectrum disorders holistically, or they want to help their children adopt healthier eating habits. Whatever your reasoning, making the decision to go gluten-free does not mean you have to sacrifice flavor or variety.

With 201 recipes, you're able to serve up kid-friendly food at every meal and have plenty on hand for snack time. Whether your kids are hungry for chicken nuggets or looking to munch on some chips, you can satisfy their cravings and feel good about what you're feeding them. Each recipe includes detailed yet easy instructions on how to whip up palate-pleasing food in no time. You'll forget you're preparing gluten-free food as quickly as they'll forget they're eating it.

Throughout, you'll also find helpful tips and tricks on how to successfully make that switch to a gluten-free lifestyle. In addition, the first chapter provides you with a more in-depth look at what it means to go gluten-free. With these recipes, hints, and additional information, you can turn your kitchen gluten-free with ease.

Making the transition to a gluten-free diet can be fun for the whole family. This book is meant to help you make that change and maintain that lifestyle. Now you can cook gluten-free meals your kids will love every day of the week!

CHAPTER 1

GLUTEN-FREE MADE EASY

This chapter will teach you how to find naturally gluten-free foods, how to spend less on your grocery bill for gluten-free foods, and how to prevent cross-contamination in your home kitchen.

GLUTEN DEFINED

Gluten is the term used for several types of proteins found in wheat, barley, and rye. The proteins gliadin and glutelin are found in these grains and together form a substance called gluten. Gluten is a "storage protein," which means that it holds the key ingredients for these grains to continue proliferating.

Gluten is primarily found in foods like bread, pasta, cakes, muffins, crackers, and pizza dough. Wheat, barley, and rye are used in many baked goods because the gluten in these grains provides excellent elasticity, structure, and texture. Gluten is what causes pizza to have a chewy, stretchy texture. It gives French bread its soft white center and chewy crust. Gluten makes cinnamon rolls stretchy, soft, and light. It helps give structure to bread dough when rising, so that the bread becomes tall and stays tall after baking and cooling.

Avoiding gluten in your children's diets can be difficult for several reasons. The biggest reason is that ingredients containing gluten are not required by law to be listed on food labels. However, by law, the top eight food allergens must be listed on every food label in the United States, and wheat (which is a primary source of gluten) is one of them. So although you may not see "gluten" in the ingredients list, you can look for food allergen information, for example, "contains wheat."

When you are removing gluten from your child's diet, you will also need to avoid these foods (most are derivatives of wheat), which also contain gluten:

- Barley
- Rye
- Triticale (a cross between rye and wheat)
- Bulgur
- Durum flour
- Farina
- Graham flour

- Kamut
- Semolina
- Spelt
- Couscous

As a matter of fact, it's often a good idea (especially when your child first receives a diagnosis of celiac disease) to only let them eat foods that are either naturally gluten-free, or actually are labeled "gluten-free" until you have a better understanding of how to read food and nutrition labels.

THE REAL DEAL ON CELIAC DISEASE AND GLUTEN SENSITIVITY

Celiac disease (also known as celiac sprue or gluten-sensitive enteropathy) is an auto-immune and digestive disorder that occurs in about one in 100 people in the United States. For children with this disorder, gluten can cause serious damage to their intestine if it is ingested. If your child has celiac disease or gluten sensitivity, gluten damages the "villi" in their intestines. Since the villi (finger-like projections that contain most of the enzymes needed for digestion) are damaged for those with celiac disease, their bodies have enormous difficulty ingesting the healthy nutrients their bodies need such as fat, calcium, iron, and folate.

Some of the symptoms of celiac disease and gluten sensitivity include:

- Digestive problems such as bloating, vomiting, excess gas and/or pain, severe and/or chronic diarrhea, irritable bowel, weight loss, weight gain, etc.
- Constant and/or severe headaches or migraines
- Low levels of iron (anemia)
- Skin rashes (also known as dermatitis herpetiformis)
- Bone or joint pain

- Depression and/or anxiety
- Seizures
- Unexplained fatigue
- Failure to thrive

Most children have a healthy immune system that prevents the body from being harmed by gluten, but for those with celiac disease the only effective treatment is avoiding foods with gluten altogether.

To get your child tested for celiac disease and/or gluten sensitivity you need to visit your family doctor or a gastroenterologist, who will do a blood test to check for high levels of certain types of antibodies. If his blood test comes back with positive results for celiac disease, the doctor may then choose to do a biopsy of his small intestine to check for damage to the villi. A diagnosis is usually given using a combination of these diagnostic tests. Gluten sensitivity (as opposed to celiac disease) is sometimes diagnosed if a patient tests negatively for the disorder, yet his or her body reacts with symptoms that are similar to those with celiac disease.

PLANNING FOR A GLUTEN-FREE LIFESTYLE

If your child has been diagnosed with celiac disease, the first thing you will want to do is gather all the information you can. Ask your pediatrician to recommend a nutritionist or registered dietitian who can give you a better understanding of what going gluten-free really means. A nutritionist may also request that your doctor order tests to help you discover if your child has any additional food sensitivities or nutritional deficiencies. These tests may include a bone scan or tests of vitamin D, calcium, iron, zinc, B12, folate, or thyroid levels. Once the doctor and nutritionist have a better picture of what's going on in your child's body, they can help determine the best plan of action and what gluten-free foods will be the most nutritious choices.

RESEARCH ONLINE

Do some online research to find local grocery stores that have gluten-free foods, along with local restaurants with gluten-free items on their menus. There are countless websites available that can help you find local gluten-free resources such as community support groups, books to help educate yourself and your family, gluten-free recipes and menus, and even gluten-free shopping guides. Your community may even have a gluten-free bakery that offers baked goods like pizza, sandwich bread, cakes, and cookies.

Stay Safe While Dining Out

Every time you visit a restaurant with your child make sure to assess the knowledge of the wait staff and kitchen staff. Ask your server for a gluten-free menu. Ask about the steps taken in the kitchen area to prevent cross-contamination. If a waiter or chef doesn't understand what gluten-free means, it may be a sign that gluten-free options are not available. Never be afraid to ask specific questions—your child's health is important!

COMMUNITY RESOURCES

One of the best places to find out about the basics of a gluten-free diet (and businesses in your community that are understanding of the gluten-free diet) is your local library. You can check out additional gluten-free cookbooks and guidebooks, do research on the public access computers, and get help from a reference librarian. Make sure to check out any local community bulletin boards to learn about gluten-free support groups that may meet in the library, local restaurants, or local church facilities. (This is also a good way to find out about churches in your area that may provide the option of gluten-free Communion or Eucharist services.)

Another great source of information is your Community or County Extension Agency. There will generally be an agent who specializes in the food resources and support groups in the community. This is also a great organization to contact if you would like to find out about regional farms that sell fresh organic produce and meats, which are usually gluten-free. These farms may also make and sell hygiene products like goat's milk soap and lotions. Often if these products are organic they typically will not contain gluten, although you will have to ask to be sure.

GLUTEN IS NOT JUST IN FOODS

Other products that can contain gluten are medications and vitamins, which may use gluten as a binder or filler. Shampoos, conditioners, toothpaste, lipsticks, and lip balms, as well as face and hand creams, can contain gluten. You will have to do your research either online or by calling companies specifically to find out which products your child uses contain gluten and which ones are safe. Gluten can't get through her skin into her bloodstream, but if she is showering, bathing, or brushing her teeth with products that contain gluten, there is a slight possibility that it could enter her mouth and her digestive system.

Gluten-Free Playtime
Children who have celiac disease can become sick from using PlayDoh, a common modeling compound made from wheat flour. Because children often put their fingers in their mouths during and after play, they can become sick from accidentally ingesting the gluten on their hands. Other alternatives include Moon Dough, which is hypoallergenic and wheat-free, and Aroma Dough, made from gluten-free flours

THE BASICS OF A GLUTEN-FREE DIET

The best part about having your child follow a basic gluten-free diet is that he'll be eating more fresh, natural, and unprocessed foods. Which means he will not only be following a gluten-free diet, but a nutritionally balanced and healthy one.

It's often recommended when starting a gluten-free diet to start with naturally gluten-free foods. These foods include:

- Fruits
- Vegetables
- Beans
- Rice
- Nuts and seeds
- Unseasoned fresh meats
- Unseasoned fresh chicken
- Fish
- Milk, cheese, and plain yogurt
- Eggs

Most of these foods (except for the beans and rice) are located around the perimeter of your grocery store, where most of the fresh foods are. Most naturally gluten-free foods will not come in a bag or box. Other than canned fruits or vegetables, rice, beans, and nuts, you can find most gluten-free foods in their natural state in the produce, meat, and dairy sections.

PANTRY MAKEOVER

The thought of having to change your family's entire diet due to celiac disease or gluten sensitivity can feel completely overwhelming. No more bread? No pasta, pizza, doughnuts, or cookies?

While this may have been true even five years ago (at least as far as purchasing these items in a local grocery store or restaurant), the gluten-free food industry has come a long way. There are many companies that produce high quality and readily available gluten-free products like sandwich breads, pastas, flours, cookies, and snacks. Most large grocery stores now have a gluten-free section, where you can find substitutions for many of your gluten-rich favorite foods.

But before you jump into buying a whole bunch of gluten-free processed foods, take a look at your kitchen. You may already have a fair amount of food that is already gluten-free. You will also need to identify foods that contain gluten, which you will need to avoid. Here is a list of naturally gluten-free foods you can keep:

- Baking ingredients such as baking powder, baking soda, salt, individual herbs and spices (not seasoning blends, which may contain gluten), oils, and sugar
- Canned, frozen, and jarred foods such as plain vegetables, beans, dried beans, fruits, peanut butter (and other nut butters), plain jams, jellies, and honey
- Canned tuna and chicken
- Plain rice (not seasoned rice mixes, which usually contain gluten)
- Fresh and frozen fruits and vegetables of all types
- Fresh and frozen unseasoned meats, chicken, and fish
- Eggs
- Natural cheeses ("cheese foods" often contain wheat)
- Milk and nondairy milk substitutions
- Unseasoned nuts

Other foods in your pantry should be moved to a designated "gluten section" or removed entirely. This includes any food that lists "flour" as an ingredient on the label. This will include most "cream of" soups, noodle soups, baking mixes, pancake mixes, all-purpose and self-rising flours, and even some nonstick baking sprays. And of course, breads, bagels, frozen pancakes, waffles, cookies, and crackers. Also off-limits are opened condiments in your fridge that family members have placed knives or spoons in (because they may have been contaminated by gluten).

Buying gluten-free specialty items can be very expensive. Gluten-free foods often cost as much as 400 percent more than their traditional wheat counterparts. For example, a loaf of regular bread may cost about $1.50, while a generally much smaller loaf of gluten-free bread can easily cost over $6.00. Because specialty gluten-free foods can be so expensive, it's cost-effective for families to eat as many naturally gluten-free foods as they can. Buying fruits and vegetables in season can help with food costs, along with purchasing canned or frozen versions during the winter months.

Another great way to save money on a gluten-free diet is to make most of your meals and snacks from scratch. Initially it might be expensive to buy gluten-free ingredients to make homemade baked goods, but they will still be cheaper than gluten-free store-bought products.

GLUTEN-FREE FLOURS AND BAKING INSTRUCTIONS

When your family's following a gluten-free diet, you not only have to learn to cook gluten-free foods, but you also need to learn how to bake without gluten. Birthday parties need cake! Big breakfasts need biscuits, or pancakes, or toast. Sandwiches need bread to hold them together.

To make these foods you will need a few special ingredients such as gluten-free flours. The gluten-free flours used in this book are brown rice flour, sorghum flour, cornstarch, and arrowroot starch. Generally you will only need two of those flours per baking recipe. Sorghum flour and millet flour can be used interchangeably in these recipes. So if you prefer millet flour over sorghum flour, feel free to substitute.

Sometimes either blanched almond flour or garbanzo bean flour are added to bread recipes, usually for sandwich-type breads. These are very high-protein flours that will help the bread structurally to rise and keep its shape after baking. Many breads need yeast to help the bread rise.

Lastly, when baking gluten-free recipes, you need a binder, which helps replace the action of gluten in baked goods. The most commonly used binder in gluten-free baking is xanthan gum. This is a powder made from a strain of bacteria that is grown on corn. When xanthan gum is introduced to a liquid, the mixture becomes thick and sticky. This quality helps give structure to gluten-free baked goods. If anyone in your family is allergic to corn products, you can use guar gum in place of the xanthan gum.

Mixing Flours

Why are so many different flours used in gluten-free baking recipes? Wheat flour has been preferred for centuries because of the special properties of gluten. Since gluten-free flours don't contain the unique elastic properties of wheat flour, they don't have the same ability to produce baked goods that are light, yet sturdy. So gluten-free baked goods often have a much better texture and taste when you combine a variety of flours that have different properties.

PREVENTING CROSS-CONTAMINATION

People with celiac disease (and often those who are gluten intolerant) will experience major symptoms if the tiniest bit of gluten comes into contact with something they ingest. The smallest amount of gluten can cause gastrointestinal distress and pain, including severe bloating, diarrhea, vomiting, constipation, stomach pain, and headaches. And these physical symptoms can last for days. Therefore, learning to keep your kitchen safe for you or your loved ones is imperative. There are many different methods you can use to prevent cross-contamination in your home.

The easiest method of preventing cross-contamination is to simply become a completely gluten-free family. Using this method, there is simply no gluten in the home to worry about. All counters will be safe. You only need one toaster and one set of cooking utensils. You won't have to worry about separating foods or accidentally using the peanut butter that nonceliac family members were using to make sandwiches. However, this option is not always financially possible or it may be difficult to convince nonceliac family members to give up foods that do not cause them harm.

Also, children and adults alike will have to learn how to contend with a gluten-eating world when they leave home. Having celiac disease or gluten sensitivity means having to learn how to navigate in the world, whether you're at a grocery store, at school, or visiting a friend's house for dinner. So having a shared kitchen can come with the benefits of learning how to adequately keep your gluten-free foods safe.

If your kitchen will contain both gluten-free and other foods, you'll need to set up a system to keep them apart. First, use separate cutting boards. Keep a gluten-free cutting board in a safe drawer on one side of the kitchen and keep another cutting board in another drawer. When preparing two types of meals, always prepare the gluten-free meals first, either on a clean surface or the gluten-free cutting board.

Use a color-coded or sticker system to differentiate gluten-free foods from gluten-containing foods. This method is especially helpful if your children aren't old enough to read yet. By placing large stickers of the same color on safe foods, it will be easy for them to tell the difference between safe and unsafe foods. Along with color-coding, teach your children and loved ones to place all gluten-free foods above gluten-containing foods in cabinets and on shelves. For example, if you have a shelf that contains regular baking ingredients, place all gluten-free baking ingredients on the shelf above the regular foods. This way you are preventing any chance of a crumb or bit of flour falling onto the gluten-free food.

When cooking gluten-free foods, you do not necessarily have to use specific pans, as long as it can be thoroughly scrubbed, washed, and sanitized in hot, soapy water. If a pan cannot be scrubbed (i.e. a nonstick pan), replace it. If you are worried about old crumbs being stuck on a particularly old pan, you can cover the pan in aluminum foil to protect the gluten-free foods from getting contaminated. However, you will need to use a designated gluten-free toaster. There is no way to completely protect against all the crumbs that have been embedded in a toaster. Try to place the separate toasters as far away from each other as possible. And as with gluten-free foods, it would be helpful to color-code the gluten-free toaster with a sticker.

While you can continue to use metal cooking utensils for gluten-free foods, you cannot use wooden utensils that have come in contact with gluten-containing foods. Gluten can get embedded in tiny grains of wooden or bamboo utensils and bowls, and therefore they cannot be used for gluten-free foods, unless they are brand-new and only used for gluten-free preparations.

For your refrigerator, buy separate condiments and label them using the color-coding system. Remember if someone placed a knife that had been on regular bread in your gluten-free mayonnaise jar, it's cross-contaminated and can no longer be considered gluten-free. Therefore, it's important to keep a special gluten-free shelf in your refrigerator. Alternately, you can buy condiments that come in plastic squeeze jars so that they never come in contact with dirty knives or spoons.

Here are the main points to remember in helping prevent cross-contamination:

- Keep separate cutting boards in designated areas.
- Prepare gluten-free foods and meals on a clean counter or cutting board before preparing gluten-containing foods.
- Use a color-coded or sticker system to mark gluten-free items.
- Make sure to wash all cooking pans thoroughly in hot, soapy water.
- If in doubt, use foil to cover baking pans to keep foods safe.
- Store gluten-free foods above gluten-containing foods in the pantry.
- Have a separate color-coded area for gluten-free condiments in the refrigerator.
- If you're concerned that gluten-free food has come in contact with gluten, stick with the adage, "If in doubt, throw it out."

GLUTEN-FREE INGREDIENTS AND WHERE TO PURCHASE THEM

Following are some common gluten-free ingredients you might want to have on hand. You might be able to find some at your grocery store—if not, look online!

INGREDIENT	WHERE TO PURCHASE
brown rice flour	bobsredmill.com, amazon.com
arrowroot starch	bobsredmill.com, amazon.com
tapioca starch/tapioca flour (these are the same thing)	bobsredmill.com, amazon.com
sorghum flour	bobsredmill.com, amazon.com
blanched almond flour	store.honeyvillegrain.com, amazon.com (brand used: Honeyville)
ground flaxseed	bobsredmill.com, amazon.com
gluten-free Bisquick	your local grocery store, amazon.com,
coconut oil	amazon.com (brand used: Nutiva Organic Extra Virgin Coconut Oil)
light (tasting) olive oil	your local grocery store, amazon.com (I recommend Bertolli Extra Light Tasting Olive Oil)
spectrum palm shortening	your local health foods store, amazon.com
xanthan gum	bobsredmill.com, amazon.com

CHAPTER 2

HOMEY BAKED GOODS

Blueberry Apple Muffins

A muffin and a yogurt make a fun and yummy lunchtime meal. If you prefer not to use the gluten-free flours listed, try using 2 cups of Gluten-Free Bisquick in its place and leave out the xanthan gum, baking powder, and salt.

MAKES 12 MUFFINS

1 cup + 2 tablespoons brown rice flour

1 cup + 2 tablespoons arrowroot starch or tapioca starch

½ teaspoon xanthan gum

1 tablespoon baking powder

½ teaspoon salt

½ teaspoon ground cinnamon

¾ cup sugar

1 cup chunky applesauce

3 tablespoons melted coconut oil or light-tasting olive oil

¾ cup milk or a nondairy alternative such as almond milk

1 teaspoon lemon juice

1 teaspoon gluten-free vanilla extract

1 cup blueberries

1. Preheat oven to 350°F. Lightly oil a standard muffin pan or line with paper liners and spritz with nonstick cooking spray.

2. In a large bowl, combine brown rice flour, arrowroot starch, xanthan gum, baking powder, salt, cinnamon, and sugar. Stir with a whisk.

3. In a small bowl whisk together applesauce, oil, milk, lemon juice, and vanilla extract.

4. Slowly mix dry ingredients into the wet.

5. Gently mix in blueberries. Make sure not to use any more than 1 cup of blueberries—if you have too many, the batter will not cook through. Spoon batter into oiled pan.

6. Bake 25–30 minutes or until a toothpick inserted into the center of a muffin comes out clean.

Cinnamon Bun Muffins

These sweet, cinnamon-filled muffins with a crumbly streusel topping are a delicious and easy addition to your morning breakfast routine. Kids love these muffins and they are easy to pack in school lunches.

MAKES 12 MUFFINS

1 cup brown rice flour

1 cup arrowroot starch or tapioca starch

2 teaspoons baking powder

1 teaspoon xanthan gum

1 tablespoon ground cinnamon

½ teaspoon sea salt

2 eggs (yolks and whites separated)

½ cup applesauce

¾ cup milk or nondairy alternative such as almond milk

¼ cup light-tasting olive oil

½ cup sugar

Cinnamon Swirl Ingredients:

1 tablespoon ground cinnamon

⅓ cup sugar

4 tablespoons melted butter or coconut oil

1. Preheat oven to 375°F. Line a muffin pan with paper liners and spritz with nonstick cooking spray. Set aside.

2. In a large bowl, whisk flour, starch, baking powder, xanthan gum, cinnamon, and salt. In a separate bowl, whisk egg yolks, applesauce, milk, oil, and sugar.

3. Add the flour mixture to the egg yolk mixture and fold just until combined. In another bowl, whip egg whites until stiff. SLOWLY fold the whipped egg whites into the muffin batter. (It's okay if you see streaks or clumps of egg white, it does NOT have to be completely incorporated!)

4. In a small bowl, mix together cinnamon swirl ingredients. Spoon muffin batter into greased or paper-lined muffin tins. To be sure your muffins have cinnamon swirls throughout, fill the muffin tin half-full, spoon on some of the cinnamon swirl and use a small knife to swirl, fill the tin with more batter, and then spoon a bit more cinnamon swirl over the top.

5. Bake for 18–25 minutes. They are done when they are golden brown and a toothpick inserted in the middle comes out clean. Cool muffins on a wire rack. Store any leftovers in an airtight container on the counter for up to 5 days.

Fluffy Cornbread

This fluffy cornbread makes a great accompaniment to soup or chili. The corn kernels add an interesting texture.

MAKES AN 8"- OR 9"-SQUARE PAN
• • • • •

1 cup gluten-free cornmeal

½ cup brown rice flour

½ cup arrowroot starch or tapioca starch

1 teaspoon xanthan gum

1 tablespoon baking powder, separated

1 teaspoon baking soda

¾ teaspoon salt

¼ cup applesauce

⅓ cup sugar

1 cup milk or nondairy alternative such as almond milk

3 tablespoons butter or coconut oil

1 cup corn kernels (fresh or frozen)

1. Preheat oven to 400°F. Oil an 8"- or 9"-square baking pan.

2. In a medium bowl, combine cornmeal, flour, arrowroot starch, xanthan gum, 2 teaspoons baking powder, baking soda, and salt.

3. In a large bowl, combine applesauce and ¼ teaspoon baking powder.

4. To applesauce mixture, add sugar, milk, and butter.

5. Slowly mix dry ingredients into wet.

6. Mix corn kernels into batter. Spread batter into prepared baking pan.

7. Bake 25–30 minutes or until a toothpick inserted into the center of the bread comes out clean.

Zucchini Muffins

You can use store-bought applesauce in this recipe as a timesaver.

MAKES 12 MUFFINS

1 cup + 2 tablespoons brown rice flour

1 cup + 2 tablespoons arrowroot starch or tapioca starch

¾ cup sugar

1 tablespoon baking powder

½ teaspoon ground cinnamon

½ teaspoon ground nutmeg

½ teaspoon xanthan gum

½ teaspoon salt

¾ cup milk or nondairy alternative such as almond milk

1 teaspoon lemon juice

1 teaspoon lemon extract

⅓ cup + 1 tablespoon applesauce

3 tablespoons melted coconut oil or light-tasting olive oil

1 cup shredded zucchini

1. Preheat oven to 350°F. Oil a standard muffin pan or line with paper liners and spritz with nonstick cooking spray.

2. In a large bowl, combine brown rice flour, arrowroot starch, sugar, baking powder, cinnamon, nutmeg, xanthan gum, and salt. Stir with a whisk.

3. In a small bowl, combine almond milk, lemon juice, lemon extract, applesauce, coconut oil, and zucchini.

4. Slowly mix dry ingredients into wet, adding one half at a time. Stir until combined. Spoon into oiled muffin pan.

5. Bake 25–30 minutes or until a toothpick inserted into the center of a muffin comes out clean.

Enticing the Picky Eater

It can be extremely frustrating if your child has limited his diet to just a few items. Trying new foods, like zucchini, in the guise of a sweet muffin can be a way to broaden your child's diet. When your child won't eat a serving of fruit or vegetables, give muffins a try!

Sweet Potato Muffins

You can use a baked sweet potato instead of canned sweet potato purée for this recipe. Peel and mash a well-cooked large sweet potato until it's smooth.

MAKES 12 MUFFINS

1 cup + 2 tablespoons brown rice flour

1 cup + 2 tablespoons arrowroot starch or tapioca starch

½ teaspoon xanthan gum

1 tablespoon baking powder

¾ teaspoon salt

1 teaspoon cinnamon

¼ teaspoon nutmeg

¼ teaspoon ground ginger

¼ cup light-tasting olive oil or melted coconut oil

1 cup packed brown sugar

1 teaspoon gluten-free vanilla extract

2 tablespoons blackstrap molasses

¾ cup milk or nondairy alternative such as almond milk

1⅓ cups sweet potato purée

1. Preheat oven to 350°F. Oil a standard muffin pan or line with paper liners and spritz with nonstick cooking spray.

2. In a large mixing bowl, combine brown rice flour, arrowroot starch, xanthan gum, baking powder, salt, and spices.

3. In a small bowl, combine oil, brown sugar, vanilla, molasses, milk, and sweet potato purée.

4. Slowly mix dry ingredients into wet. Spoon into prepared muffin pan.

5. Bake 18–23 minutes, or until a toothpick inserted into the center of a muffin comes out clean.

Keep Your Cool, Xanthan Gum

Xanthan gum is a great tool for gluten-free baking, as it helps the nonglutinous flour ingredients stick together. However, you only need a little bit in any given recipe, so one package can last a long time. To maximize the life of your xanthan gum, keep it in the freezer. Well packaged and kept cold, xanthan gum can last for up to 6 months.

Cranberry Oatmeal Cookies

If you're craving a tasty cookie but don't have any cranberries on hand, substitute raisins or another gluten-free dried fruit.

MAKES 48 COOKIES
••••••••••••••••••••

½ cup brown rice flour

½ cup arrowroot starch or tapioca starch

1 teaspoon xanthan gum

2 cups gluten-free old-fashioned rolled oats

½ teaspoon cinnamon

½ teaspoon baking soda

½ teaspoon salt

¼ cup applesauce

¼ teaspoon baking powder

½ cup packed dark brown sugar

¼ cup pure maple syrup

½ cup light-tasting olive oil or melted coconut oil

½ cup dried, sweetened cranberries (gluten-free)

½ cup gluten-free chocolate chips (optional)

1. Preheat oven to 350°F.

2. In a medium bowl, combine brown rice flour, arrowroot starch, xanthan gum, oats, cinnamon, baking soda, and salt. Stir with a whisk to combine.

3. In a large bowl, combine applesauce with baking powder. Add brown sugar, maple syrup, and oil.

4. Mix dry ingredients into wet.

5. Stir in cranberries and chocolate chips, if using.

6. Drop by tablespoon-full onto ungreased cookie sheets.

7. Bake 13–15 minutes or until golden brown. Remove to cooling rack to cool.

Is Pure Maple Syrup Important?

Yes. Many "pancake syrups" are mixtures of several ingredients. They can include gluten-containing ingredients. Pure maple syrup comes from maple trees and does not contain gluten.

Strawberry Cranberry Muffins

If you are going to use frozen strawberries, thaw them and drain off any extra juice before using in this recipe.

MAKES 12 MUFFINS

1 cup + 2 tablespoons brown rice flour or oat flour

1 cup + 2 tablespoons arrowroot starch or tapioca starch

¾ cup sugar

1 tablespoon baking powder

½ teaspoon xanthan gum

½ teaspoon salt

¾ cup milk or nondairy alternative such as almond milk

1 teaspoon lemon juice

1 teaspoon almond extract

⅓ cup + 1 tablespoon applesauce

3 tablespoons melted coconut oil or light-tasting olive oil

½ cup chopped strawberries

½ cup dried cranberries

1. Preheat oven to 350°F. Oil a standard muffin pan or line with paper liners and spritz with nonstick cooking spray.

2. In a large bowl, whisk together brown rice flour, arrowroot starch, sugar, baking powder, xanthan gum, and salt.

3. In a medium bowl mix together milk, lemon juice, almond extract, applesauce, and oil.

4. Stir the wet ingredients into the dry ingredients to create a wet batter.

5. Fold chopped strawberries and cranberries into batter. Spoon batter into muffin pan, filling ¾ full.

6. Bake 20–25 minutes, or until a toothpick inserted into the center of a muffin comes out clean. Remove to a cooling rack and cool completely.

Are Oats Okay for a Gluten-Free Diet?

Check with your doctor before including gluten-free oats in your diet. Oats do not contain gluten, but oats that are not labeled "gluten free" are probably contaminated with other gluten-containing grains through the growing, milling, or packaging process. For many people who follow a gluten-free diet, doctors feel that gluten-free oats are a safe whole grain. If you need to avoid oats completely, try using 1 cup sorghum flour and 1 cup brown rice flour in this recipe instead of oat flour.

Basic Crepes

Making crepes takes a little practice to perfect your flipping technique, but they still taste very delicious while you're working on your style.

MAKES 4 CREPES

¼ cup milk or almond milk

¼ cup water

2 tablespoons plus 1 teaspoon melted butter or coconut oil, divided

½ cup brown rice flour

¼ teaspoon xanthan gum

⅛ teaspoon salt

1. In a small or medium bowl, combine milk, water, and 2 tablespoons melted butter.
2. Add remaining ingredients except butter and stir with a fork until smooth.
3. Brush a 5" or 6" skillet with remaining melted butter and heat over medium-high flame.
4. Pour approximately 3 tablespoons of batter into pan, swirling batter.
5. Once edges are set, flip with a pancake turner and cook on other side.
6. Place cooked crepes on waxed paper to cool.

Maple Cinnamon Crepes

These sweet crepes are perfect filled with Strawberry Applesauce (Chapter 3), or sliced bananas.

MAKES 4 CREPES

¼ cup milk or almond milk

¼ cup water

2 tablespoons plus 1 teaspoon melted butter or coconut oil, divided

1 tablespoon pure maple syrup

½ cup brown rice flour

¼ teaspoon xanthan gum

⅛ teaspoon salt

¼ teaspoon cinnamon

1. In a small or medium bowl, combine milk, water, 2 tablespoons melted butter, and maple syrup.
2. Add remaining ingredients except butter and stir with a fork until smooth.
3. Brush a 5" or 6" skillet with remaining melted butter, and heat over medium-high flame.
4. Pour approximately 3 tablespoons of batter into pan, swirling batter.
5. Once edges are set, flip with a pancake turner and cook on other side.
6. Place cooked crepes on waxed paper to cool.

Old-Fashioned Biscuits

This recipe is for drop biscuits, but you can also roll out the dough and cut out the biscuits with a cookie cutter.

MAKES 6–8 BISCUITS

1 cup brown rice flour

1 cup arrowroot starch or tapioca starch

1 teaspoon xanthan gum

1 tablespoon baking powder

½ teaspoon salt

½ cup butter or coconut oil

½ cup milk or almond milk

2 eggs or 1 tablespoon EnerG Egg Replacer mixed with 4 tablespoons warm water

1. Preheat oven to 425°F.

2. In a medium bowl, combine flour, arrowroot startch, xanthan gum, baking powder, and salt.

3. Cut butter into flour mixture with either a pastry cutter or two knives.

4. Mix in milk and eggs; and continue to stir until you have a thick biscuit dough.

5. Using a greased ice-cream scoop, place scoops of dough 2" apart on a greased or parchment paper lined cookie sheet.

6. Bake 12–15 minutes or until golden and crusty.

Chocolate Chip Mini Muffins

These muffins are a great treat, and their little size makes them easy to take along when you're on the go.

MAKES 24 MUFFINS

1 cup + 2 tablespoons brown rice flour

1 cup + 2 tablespoons arrowroot starch or tapioca starch

¾ cup brown sugar

1 tablespoon baking powder

½ teaspoon xanthan gum

½ teaspoon salt

¾ cup milk or nondairy alternative like almond milk

2 teaspoons gluten-free vanilla extract

⅓ cup + 1 tablespoon applesauce

3 tablespoons melted coconut oil or light-tasting olive oil

1 cup Enjoy Life allergen-free mini chocolate chips

1. Preheat oven to 350°F. Oil a mini muffin pan or line with paper liners and spritz with nonstick cooking spray.

2. In a large bowl whisk together brown rice flour, arrowroot starch, brown sugar, baking powder, xanthan gum, and salt.

3. In a medium bowl whisk together milk, vanilla extract, applesauce, and oil.

4. Mix dry ingredients into wet, one half at a time.

5. Stir chocolate chips into batter. Spoon batter into oiled muffin pan.

6. Cook 12–15 minutes or until a toothpick inserted into the center of a muffin comes out clean.

Mixed Berry Muffins

In summer, substitute fresh berries. Any combination of raspberries, blueberries, blackberries, or strawberries works really well in this recipe.

MAKES 12 MUFFINS

1 cup + 2 tablespoons brown rice flour

1 cup + 2 tablespoons arrowroot starch or tapioca starch

¾ cup brown sugar

1 tablespoon baking powder

½ teaspoon xanthan gum

½ teaspoon salt

¾ cup milk or nondairy alternative like almond milk

1 teaspoon lemon juice

1 teaspoon gluten-free almond extract

⅓ cup + 1 tablespoon applesauce

3 tablespoons melted coconut oil or light-tasting olive oil

1 cup fresh or frozen mixed berries, chopped

1. Preheat oven to 350°F. Oil a standard muffin pan or line with paper liners and spritz with nonstick cooking spray.

2. In a large bowl whisk together brown rice flour, arrowroot starch, sugar, baking powder, xanthan gum, and salt.

3. In a smaller bowl mix together milk, lemon juice, almond extract, applesauce, and oil.

4. Mix dry ingredients into wet, one half at a time.

5. Stir in berries. (If using frozen berries, *do not* thaw them beforehand or they will melt into the batter and turn the batter purple.) Spoon batter into muffin pan.

6. Bake 25–30 minutes or until a toothpick inserted into the center of a muffin comes out clean.

PB & J Muffins

These muffins are a great alternative to peanut butter and jelly sandwiches. When gluten-free bread doesn't pack well, these muffins make a great stand-in. If you cannot tolerate gluten-free oats, use 1 cup brown rice flour and 1 cup of arrowroot starch in place of the oat flour.

MAKES 12 MUFFINS

1 cup + 2 tablespoons brown rice flour or oat flour

1 cup + 2 tablespoons arrowroot starch or tapioca starch

1 tablespoon baking powder

½ teaspoon xanthan gum

½ teaspoon salt

¾ cup brown sugar

⅓ cup + 1 tablespoon peanut butter or almond butter

3 tablespoons melted coconut oil or light-tasting olive oil

1 cup milk or nondairy alternative such as almond milk

2 teaspoons gluten-free vanilla extract

1 cup chopped raspberries or strawberries

1. Preheat oven to 350°F. Oil a standard muffin pan or line with paper cupcake liners and spritz with nonstick cooking spray.

2. In a large bowl whisk together brown rice flour, arrowroot starch, baking powder, xanthan gum, and salt.

3. In a smaller bowl, cream together brown sugar, peanut butter, and oil. Slowly stir in milk and vanilla extract and whisk to combine until creamy. Pour the wet ingredient mixture into the dry ingredients and stir until you have a thick batter.

4. Fold in chopped raspberries or strawberries. Spoon batter into oiled muffin pan.

5. Bake 25–30 minutes or until a toothpick inserted into the center of a muffin comes out clean.

Pumpkin Spice Muffins

These muffins are so delicious that if you top them with Vanilla Frosting (Chapter 10) they can pass as cupcakes.

MAKES 12 MUFFINS

1 cup + 2 tablespoons brown rice flour

1 cup + 2 tablespoons arrowroot starch or tapioca starch

½ teaspoon xanthan gum

1 tablespoon baking powder

¾ teaspoon salt

1½ teaspoons cinnamon

½ teaspoon nutmeg

½ cup milk or nondairy alternative such as almond milk

3 tablespoons light-tasting olive oil or melted coconut oil

1 cup packed dark brown sugar

1 teaspoon gluten-free vanilla

¾ cup solid-packed pure pumpkin purée

½ cup dried cherries or raisins, optional

1. Preheat oven to 350°F. Line a standard muffin pan with cupcake papers and spritz with nonstick cooking spray.

2. In a large bowl, combine brown rice flour, arrowroot starch, xanthan gum, 1 tablespoon baking powder, salt, cinnamon, and nutmeg.

3. In a separate bowl, combine oil, brown sugar, vanilla, and pumpkin. Stir until smooth.

4. Mix dry ingredients into wet, one half at a time.

5. If desired, stir dried cherries or raisins into batter. Spoon batter into greased cupcake liners.

6. Bake 18–23 minutes or until a toothpick inserted into the center of a muffin comes out clean.

Fresh Muffins Taste Best

Gluten-free muffins that are made without eggs are slightly more fragile than traditional muffins. They taste best fresh from the oven, but will keep for up to 3 days in a sealed container. They can also be frozen for up to 2 months. To best enjoy muffins after the first day, warm them before serving.

Basic Pie and Tart Pastry

A versatile easy recipe for a homemade gluten-free pie crust. It does take a little practice to learn how to roll out dough, but because this crust doesn't contain gluten, you can never overwork the dough!

**MAKES 1 8" OR 9" PIE CRUST
OR TART PASTRY**
. . . .
¾ cup sorghum flour

¾ cup arrowroot starch

½ teaspoon sea salt

¼ teaspoon xanthan gum

½ cup Spectrum Palm Shortening

1 large egg

2 tablespoons ice-cold water, as needed

1. In a large bowl, whisk together sorghum flour, arrowroot starch, salt, and xanthan gum. Using a pastry blender or a knife and fork, cut in shortening throughout the flour until it resembles small peas. Make a well in the center of the flour and add the egg and 1 tablespoon of ice-cold water. Mix with a fork until the dough gathers up into a ball. Shape dough into a round disk, cover with plastic wrap, and refrigerate dough for at least 1 hour.

2. Place 2 large sheets of plastic wrap, wax paper, or parchment paper onto a large flat surface, like your countertop. Liberally sprinkle sorghum flour over the entire surface. Place another sheet of plastic wrap on top of the dough (to keep it from sticking to the rolling pin) and roll out dough until it is about ⅛" and about 11"–13" across. Once the dough has been rolled out, gently roll the dough onto the rolling pin to transfer it to the pie pan. (Or, for an easier method of rolling out gluten-free pie crust, check out this blog post with a great instructional video: *http://bit.ly/h2Ttet.*)

3. Gently unroll the crust into the pan. It's okay if the dough cracks and doesn't transfer perfectly. This dough is very forgiving and you simply patch up the dough with your fingers. Cut off any extra dough around the pan and flute the edges of the crust. You can also simply mark the edges with a fork for a rustic look. Another option is to reroll out the scraps of dough and cut out shapes with cookie cutters; then you can decoratively place the shapes on top of your pie filling right before baking. Now the unbaked crust is ready for making a pie.

4. For a prebaked crust: Heat oven to 350°F and prick small holes in the bottom of the crust with a fork. Bake for 10–15 minutes until crust is golden brown.

Basic Sandwich Bread

This easy and delicious gluten-free yeast bread recipe uses as few ingredients as possible.

**MAKES 1 (8½" × 4½") LOAF
OF GLUTEN-FREE BREAD**
• •

1 cup brown rice flour

1 cup arrowroot starch or tapioca starch

3 tablespoons ground flaxseeds

3 tablespoons gluten-free rolled oats

½ teaspoon salt

1½ teaspoons xanthan gum

2 teaspoons SAF-Instant Yeast, Red Star Quick-Rise or Bread Machine Yeast, or Fleischmann's Bread Machine Yeast

3 tablespoons sugar or honey

2 large eggs, room temperature

1 cup plus 2 tablespoons milk or almond milk, heated to 110°F

2 tablespoons olive oil

1. In a large bowl whisk together brown rice flour, arrowroot starch, ground flaxseeds, oats, salt, xanthan gum, yeast, and sugar. In a smaller bowl whisk together eggs, milk, and olive oil.

2. Pour wet ingredients into dry ingredients. Stir with a wooden spoon or a fork for several minutes until batter resembles a thick cake batter. First it will look like biscuit dough, but after a few minutes it will appear thick and sticky.

3. Line an 8½" × 4½" metal or glass loaf pan with parchment paper or spritz generously with nonstick cooking spray. Pour bread dough into the pan. Using a spatula that's been dipped in water or spritzed with oil or nonstick cooking spray, spread the dough evenly in the pan. Continue to use the spatula to smooth out the top of the dough.

4. Cover the pan with a tea towel or cover loosely with plastic wrap that has been spritzed with nonstick spray or olive oil (so it will not stick to the dough). Allow dough to rise in a warm space for 1–2 hours until doubled in size. The top of the loaf should rise about 1" above the lip of the pan.

5. Once your dough has doubled, preheat the oven to 425°F. Remove the covering from the loaf and bake for 25–35 minutes. If the bread begins to brown more than desired, place a sheet of foil over the loaf and continue baking. The bread will be done when the internal temperature is between 190–200°F, when tested with a food thermometer. Allow bread to cool completely on a wire rack for 2–3 hours before slicing. If you slice the bread when it is still hot, it may lose its shape and fall.

6. Bread will keep on the counter in a zip-top plastic bag for 2–3 days. After 3 days, slice and freeze the remaining loaf.

Best Pizza Crust

A crusty, thick, and chewy pizza dough that, believe it or not, is gluten-free!

MAKES 2 12" PIZZA CRUSTS

2 cups brown rice flour

2 cups arrowroot starch or tapioca starch

⅔ cup blanched almond flour or nonfat dry milk powder

1 teaspoon salt

1 tablespoon sugar

3 teaspoons xanthan gum

2 teaspoons Saf Instant-Yeast, Red Star Rapid Rise or "Bread Machine" Yeast, or Fleischmann's "Bread Machine" Yeast

1½ cups water, warmed to 110 degrees

4 egg whites, room temperature

3 tablespoons olive oil

½ teaspoon apple cider vinegar

Optional: 1 teaspoon Italian seasoning, for adding to pizza dough

Optional: ½ teaspoon garlic salt and additional olive oil for sprinkling over pizza dough

1. In a large bowl, whisk together brown rice flour, arrowroot starch, blanched almond flour, salt, sugar, xanthan gum, and yeast. If desired, add Italian seasoning to the flour mixture. In a smaller bowl, whisk together the water, egg whites, olive oil, and apple cider vinegar.

2. Pour wet ingredients into whisked dry ingredients. Stir with a wooden spoon or a fork for several minutes until batter resembles a thick cake batter. First, it will look like biscuit dough, but after a few minutes it will appear thick and sticky.

3. Line 2 (12") pizza pans with parchment paper or spritz generously with nonstick cooking spray. Divide pizza dough in half and place dough in the center of each pizza pan. Place a piece of plastic wrap over the dough and gently pat the dough out into an 11" or 12" pizza crust. Leave the crust edges a little bit higher than the center of the dough, so they can contain the sauce and fillings.

4. Cover the pizza dough loosely with plastic wrap that has been spritzed with nonstick spray or olive oil (so it will not stick to the dough if it touches it). Allow the pizza dough to rise in a warm space for 10–20 minutes. Preheat oven to 400°F.

5. Remove the plastic wrap from the dough. Pre-bake dough for 10–15 minutes before adding toppings, fillings, and cheese. Finish baking pizza for an additional 15–20 minutes until cheese is melted and fillings are heated through.

6. Allow pizza to cool for 10–15 minutes before slicing and serving.

CHAPTER 3

WHAT'S FOR BREAKFAST?

Banana Yogurt Milkshake

Agave nectar or honey can be used to sweeten this to your taste. Use different flavored yogurts to make different flavored milkshakes. Blending up crushed ice in the milkshake creates a thicker shake.

MAKES 2 CUPS

1 banana

1 tablespoon lemon juice

8 ounces vanilla yogurt or nondairy yogurt such as So Delicious Coconut Milk Yogurt

1 cup milk or nondairy alternative such as almond milk

1 tablespoon ground flaxseeds

Combine all ingredients in a blender until smooth.

Blueberry and Banana Yogurt with Crispy Rice

Yogurt gets a nutrition and texture boost with fresh banana and crispy rice.

MAKES 2 CUPS

½ ripe banana

8 ounces blueberry yogurt or nondairy alternative such as So Delicious Coconut Milk Yogurt

¼ cup gluten-free crispy rice cereal

1. In a medium bowl, mash banana with a fork.
2. Combine with blueberry yogurt.
3. Stir in crispy rice cereal and serve.

Granola

Making your own granola can open up cereal options for your child. Check with your doctor to make sure gluten-free oats are okay for your child.

MAKES 10 SERVINGS

2 cups gluten-free oats

⅓ cup chopped pecans

¼ cup chopped almonds

¼ cup apple juice

¼ cup pure maple syrup

2 tablespoons light-tasting olive oil or melted coconut oil

1 teaspoon cinnamon

½ cup dried apple slices, chopped

1. Preheat oven to 350°F. Oil a cookie sheet.

2. In a large bowl, combine oats, nuts, apple juice, maple syrup, oil, and cinnamon.

3. Spread mixture on cookie sheet. Bake 15–20 minutes or until golden brown.

4. When cool, combine with dried apples. Store in an airtight container in your pantry for up to 2 weeks.

Mix It Up!

Using different dried fruits in your granola can really change the flavor. Try dried cherries, raisins, or even dried blueberries in your granola. Changing nuts can also shake up the flavor. Cashews, walnuts, or even sunflower and pumpkin seeds can all make a yummy granola.

Blueberry Syrup for Waffles

This syrup is sweetened only with fruit juice and blueberries. It's delicious served over gluten-free pancakes, waffles, or coffee cake, or you could even stir it into a fruit smoothie or a cup of hot green tea.

MAKES 2 CUPS

2 cups blueberries

⅓ cup apple juice concentrate

1 tablespoon cornstarch

2 tablespoons cold water

1. In a small saucepan, combine blueberries and apple juice concentrate. Simmer 10 minutes.

2. While the fruit is simmering, combine cornstarch and water in a small bowl.

3. Add cornstarch mixture to blueberries. Simmer and stir continuously, until thickened. Store cooled syrup in a covered glass jar in the refrigerator for up to 2 weeks.

Blueberries on Ice

Freezing blueberries at home is a great way to make the taste of summer last all year. Wash the blueberries, dry them, and pick out any damaged berries. Then, spread the berries out on a cookie sheet and freeze. Once frozen solid, transfer the berries to a freezer-safe container, where they can be enjoyed for up to 1 year.

Baked Chocolate Doughnuts

One of the things your kids might miss most when on a gluten-free diet is doughnuts. These quick doughnuts are baked, making them a (slightly) healthier option.

SERVES 6
••••••••••

Doughnut Ingredients:

¾ cup brown rice flour

¼ cup + 1 tablespoon arrowroot starch

½ teaspoon xanthan gum

3 tablespoons cocoa powder

½ cup white sugar

1 teaspoon baking powder

¼ teaspoon salt

2 large eggs

¼ cup light-tasting olive oil

¼ cup almond milk

½ teaspoon apple cider vinegar

Frosting Ingredients:

1 cup confectioners' sugar

2 tablespoons cocoa powder

2 tablespoons butter or coconut oil, softened

1–2 tablespoons almond milk

1. Preheat your oven to 375°F. Lightly grease a doughnut pan.

2. In a large bowl, whisk together all the dry ingredients.

3. In a smaller bowl, whisk together all the wet ingredients.

4. Pour the wet ingredients into the dry ingredients and stir until fully combined.

5. Spoon mixture into prepared doughnut pan. Bake in preheated oven for 10–12 minutes, or until a toothpick inserted into the thickest part of the doughnut comes out clean.

6. Let doughnuts sit for 5 minutes before turning them out onto a cooling rack. Allow to cool completely before frosting.

7. For the frosting: stir together the confectioners' sugar, 2 tablespoons cocoa powder, butter, and enough milk to make the glaze the consistency you want. Dip your cooled doughnuts into the glaze, and top with sprinkles, chopped nuts, or shredded coconut, if desired.

Cantaloupe Papaya Smoothie

This smoothie is a vibrant orange color. It pleases the eyes as well as the taste buds.

MAKES 2¼ CUPS

1 cup frozen cantaloupe chunks

½ cup frozen papaya chunks

½ cup orange juice

1 cup milk or nondairy alternative such as almond milk

Combine all ingredients in a blender until smooth.

Fresh Fruit Slush

This tangy mixture can be used as a light dip for fruit or as a dressing to drizzle over fresh fruit. Frozen mangos and strawberries can also be used together as an alternative to peaches.

YIELDS 3 CUPS

1 (10-ounce) package frozen unsweetened peach slices, thawed

1 (10-ounce) package frozen unsweetened sliced strawberries, thawed

2 tablespoons sugar or honey

1 tablespoon lemon juice

1 teaspoon lime juice

¼ teaspoon gluten-free vanilla extract

1. Combine all ingredients in a food processor.
2. Process until smooth.

Fruit Kabobs

Using plastic straws instead of sharp toothpicks or skewers makes this a treat safer for young children to enjoy.

MAKES 4 KABOBS

¼ cup cantaloupe cubes

¼ cup honeydew cubes

¼ cup pineapple cubes

¼ cup peach cubes

Small plastic straws (or drink stirrers)

1. Cut each fruit into 1" cubes.
2. Thread cubes onto the straw, alternating fruits.

Have Fun with Food!

Creating playful presentations can be fun for parents and children alike. Making smiley-face pancakes using artfully arranged blueberries or creating a flower out of fruit salad can make meal-time a happy time for everyone.

Mixed Fruit and Yogurt Smoothie

Feel free to substitute other fruits in this recipe, such as honeydew, strawberries, or bananas.

MAKES 5 CUPS

1 cup frozen cantaloupe chunks

1 cup frozen pineapple pieces

1 cup frozen blueberries

1 cup yogurt or nondairy alternative such as So Delicious Coconut Milk Yogurt

1 cup milk or nondairy alternative such as almond milk

1 cup apple juice

1. Combine all ingredients in a blender.
2. Blend until smooth.

Oatmeal with Cinnamon Apples

If your doctor has determined that it would be best to avoid oats, other gluten-free grains such as quinoa, teff seeds, or brown rice would work really well in place of the oats.

MAKES 2 CUPS

½ cup water

½ cup apple juice

1 Golden Delicious apple, cored and chopped

⅔ cup gluten-free rolled oats

1 teaspoon ground cinnamon

3–4 tablespoons sugar

1 cup milk or nondairy alternative such as almond milk

1. In a small saucepan, combine water, apple juice, and apple pieces. Bring to a boil.

2. Once boiling, stir in rolled oats and cinnamon. Return to a boil.

3. Reduce heat down to low and simmer to desired thickness, 3–5 minutes.

4. Add sugar to reach desired sweetness.

5. Pour milk over oatmeal and serve.

Orange Pineapple Smoothie

The vitamin C–rich combination of orange and pineapple tastes bright and refreshing and is a perfect way to jumpstart a gloomy day!

MAKES 2¼ CUPS

1 cup frozen pineapple chunks

½ frozen banana

¾ cup orange juice

¾ cup milk or nondairy alternative such as almond milk

Combine all ingredients in a blender until smooth.

Why a Frozen Banana?

Using a frozen banana helps improve the texture of this drink and makes it more smoothie-like. To make a frozen banana, just peel a ripe banana, place it in a zip-top bag, and freeze overnight.

Peach Raspberry Compote

Serve this easy compote with a hot cereal like grits or on top of gluten-free toasted waffles.

MAKES 2 CUPS

1 cup chopped peaches

1 cup raspberries

2 tablespoons apple juice concentrate

In a large saucepan, simmer all ingredients together until fruit starts to soften and break down, approximately 10 minutes. Allow compote to cool on the stove for at least 15–20 minutes before serving. Store any leftovers in a sealed glass jar in the refrigerator for up to 2 weeks.

What a Peach!

The peach, a sweet vitamin-rich summer fruit, is so delightful that Americans use its name to conjure up all kinds of positive images. From the complimentary, "She's a peach," to the upbeat, "I'm feeling peachy," the peach has become a synonym for sweetness. Although the nectarine is a smooth-skinned variety of peach, you just don't hear anyone saying, "You're such a nectarine!"

Strawberry Applesauce

Strawberries provide a pretty and fun addition to traditional applesauce, especially in early summer when fresh strawberries are in season.

MAKES 2 CUPS

1 cup peeled and diced apples

1 cup cut strawberries

¼ cup apple juice

1. In a medium saucepan, combine all ingredients.
2. Cover and simmer for about 10–15 minutes, until fruit is tender.
3. Mash with potato masher or purée in blender to desired consistency. When sauce has cooled, store any leftovers in a sealed glass jar in the refrigerator for up to 2 weeks.

I Like to Eat, Eat, Eat...Apples and Carrots!

Apples are a popular food to mix other foods with. Many fruits combined with apples will create wonderful "sauces." Try unique combinations of fruits and vegetables. For example, create a mixed berry applesauce using blackberries and blueberries. Whip up an orange applesauce, or even try a carrot applesauce!

Pink Milk

This recipe is absolutely delicious with a nondairy milk such as Blue Diamond Almond Breeze. If the milk isn't quite sweet enough for your child to enjoy, stir in a few tablespoons of honey after blending.

MAKES 2 CUPS
....
2 cups milk or nondairy alternative such as almond milk

¼ cup chopped strawberries

Combine all ingredients in a blender until smooth. Store any leftovers in a sealed glass jar in the refrigerator for up to 1 week.

Boost the Vitamins While Boosting Flavor!
Blending strawberries, blueberries, peaches, or pineapple with milk can make getting your calcium a treat. Fresh or frozen fruits add a burst of color, sweetness, and vitamins.

Strawberry Banana Yogurt

Add some texture to this smooth breakfast by mixing in dried fruit or cereal.

MAKES 2 CUPS
....
1 cup yogurt or nondairy alternative such as So Delicious Coconut Milk Yogurt

½ cup sliced strawberries

½ sliced banana

½ teaspoon cinnamon

Combine all ingredients in a bowl and mix well with a spoon. Store any leftovers in a sealed glass jar in the refrigerator for up to 1 week.

Strawberry Blueberry Banana Smoothie

This smoothie has a delightful purple hue.

MAKES 2¼ CUPS

½ cup frozen strawberries

½ cup frozen blueberries

½ frozen banana

½ cup apple juice

1 cup milk or nondairy alternative such
as almond milk

Combine all ingredients in a blender until smooth. Store any leftovers in a sealed glass jar in the refrigerator for up to 1 week.

Strawberry Topping

This is a very simple low-sugar topping for sorbet, gluten-free waffles, or hot cereal. If you prefer a sweeter strawberry sauce, stir in 3 tablespoons of honey while cooking.

MAKES 1 CUP

1 cup chopped strawberries

¼ cup water

1. In a small saucepan, combine strawberries and water.

2. Cook over medium heat, breaking up strawberries with the back of a spoon as they cook. Cook for 10–15 minutes until water has reduced by half.

3. Serve warm or at room temperature. Store any leftovers in a sealed glass jar in the refrigerator for up to 2 weeks.

Sunflower-Seed Butter and Banana Smoothie

This smoothie provides protein, calcium, and potassium in the guise of a sweet frozen treat.

MAKES 4 CUPS

1½ frozen bananas

⅓ cup sunflower-seed butter (one popular brand is Sunbutter)

⅓ cup apple juice

2 cups milk or nondairy alternative such as almond milk

2 teaspoons sugar or honey

1. Combine all ingredients in a blender.

2. Blend until smooth. Store any leftovers in a sealed glass jar in the refrigerator for up to 1 week.

Sunflower Seeds Not Just for the Birds

Sunflower seeds, the mainstay of many wild bird feeders and baseball pitchers, are a great source of nutrition for your family. They are great sources of vitamin E and folate, plus a host of minerals. They are also a good source of protein and good fats. So, grind some up into sunflower-seed butter and add them to your recipes for a creamy, health-improving boost.

Easy Veggie Scramble

To make this quick entrée even more convenient, use thawed frozen chopped spinach. If you or your child cannot tolerate eggs, make this a bean and veggie scramble instead by using 2 cups of cooked white or black beans in place of the scrambled eggs.

**MAKES 3 SERVINGS
(¾ CUP PER SERVING)**
. . . .

4 tablespoons olive oil, divided

6 large eggs

1 minced garlic clove

½ cup minced onion

1 cup chopped spinach

1 tablespoon gluten-free soy sauce or soy-free alternative like Coconut Secret Coconut Aminos

1. In a large skillet or sauté pan, heat 2 tablespoons of olive oil over medium-high heat. While oil is heating, in a small bowl whisk together eggs. When oil is hot, pour eggs into pan. Stir constantly for 2–3 minutes until eggs are fully scrambled and cooked. Remove eggs from pan, place in a clean bowl, and set aside.

2. Heat remaining 2 tablespoons of olive oil over medium-high heat. Sauté garlic and onion until soft, golden, and fragrant, about 3–4 minutes.

3. Add spinach, and sauté until wilted.

4. Return scrambled eggs to skillet and add soy sauce or Coconut Aminos.

5. Continue to cook over medium-high heat until heated through, approximately 2–3 minutes. Serve with fresh fruit and gluten-free toast.

Tropical Fruit Smoothie

This summery treat is loaded with vitamins A and C.

**MAKES 2 SERVINGS
(1¼ CUPS PER SERVING)**

½ cup frozen pineapple chunks

½ cup frozen mango chunks

½ cup frozen strawberries

1 cup milk or nondairy alternative such as almond milk

½ cup orange juice

Combine all ingredients in a blender until smooth. Store any leftovers in a sealed glass jar in the refrigerator for up to 2 weeks.

Smoothie Tricks and Tips

Not all children are comfortable with the feeling of cold smoothie on their lips. Don't give up after the first attempt. Straws can be helpful for some children. Another thing to try is to blend a thicker smoothie and serve it with a spoon.

Skillet Breakfast

Serve this skillet alone or topped with scrambled eggs or cooked white beans.

SERVES 4

1 bell pepper, chopped

½ onion, chopped

6 button mushrooms, chopped

1 clove garlic, minced

3 tablespoons olive oil

3 medium white potatoes, cooked and diced

1 tomato, chopped

1. In a skillet over medium heat, sauté pepper, onion, mushrooms, and garlic in olive oil until tender, about 5 minutes.

2. Add potatoes and cook until potatoes are browned, about 8–10 minutes.

3. Add tomato and cook until mixture is heated through, 2–3 minutes.

Sunday Morning Pancakes

Pancakes are a weekend tradition in many families and just because you're gluten-free doesn't mean you can't enjoy them too. These easy pancakes will be a favorite addition to your breakfast routine and can even be used as a gluten-free wrap for sandwiches in a pinch.

MAKES 10–14 PANCAKES, DEPENDING ON SIZE

1 cup sorghum flour

½ cup arrowroot starch

2½ teaspoons baking powder

1 teaspoon sugar

½ teaspoon sea salt

¼ teaspoon xanthan gum (optional, will help thicken the batter)

2 teaspoons gluten-free vanilla extract

1 cup almond milk

1 large egg

2 tablespoons light-tasting olive oil

1. In a medium bowl whisk together the sorghum flour, arrowroot starch, baking powder, sugar, sea salt, and xanthan gum, if using. Make a well in the center of the dry ingredients and add the vanilla, almond milk, egg, and olive oil. Whisk together until you have a thickened batter.

2. Grease a large heavy-bottomed skillet or nonstick pan with olive oil or nonstick spray. Heat pan on medium-high heat until it's hot enough to make a drop of water sizzle. Pour a few tablespoons up to ¼ cup of batter per pancake.

3. Cook until bubbles form on the top and pop and the edges are slightly dry. Flip with a spatula and cook the opposite side for 1–2 minutes.

4. Serve piping hot with butter or coconut oil and real maple syrup!

Make Hearty, Whole-Grain Pancakes

If you would like to add more fiber to these delicious pancakes, simply add 3 tablespoons of gluten-free rolled oats and 2–3 tablespoons of ground flaxseeds. Both will add fiber and plant protein, and the ground flaxseeds add heart-healthy omega-3 fatty acids.

Crispy Potato Pancakes

This is basically a good, old kosher recipe. It is marvelous with applesauce, sour cream, or both. For an easy brunch, it's excellent with eggs on the side.

MAKES ABOUT 10 PANCAKES

4 Idaho potatoes, peeled and coarsely grated

2 mild onions, chopped fine

2 eggs, well beaten

½ cup brown rice flour

Salt and pepper, to taste

2 cups light-tasting olive oil

Applesauce, fruit preserves, salsa, or chutney for garnish

1. In a large bowl, mix the grated potatoes, onions, and eggs together. Sprinkle with brown rice flour, salt, and pepper.

2. Heat the oil to 350°F and spoon in the potato cakes, pressing down to make a patty.

3. Fry until golden, about 5 minutes per side. Drain, keep warm, and serve with garnish of choice. These pancakes are best freshly made; however, leftovers can be stored in an airtight container in the refrigerator for up to 1 week.

The Origins of Potato Pancakes

During the long winters in northern and eastern Europe, when fresh fruits and vegetables were not available, winter storage of carrots, potatoes, beets, Brussels sprouts, apples, and dried fruits was crucial to prevent scurvy, or ascorbic acid deficiency. As Mother Nature would have it, these vegetables are packed with vitamins and minerals. Potato pancakes with applesauce or fruit syrups became a staple in harsh climates.

Fresh Mushroom Scramble

Simple and fresh ingredients come together to create this tasty and satisfying breakfast scramble.

SERVES 4–6

4 egg whites

8 whole eggs

2 tablespoons milk or nondairy alternative such as unsweetened almond milk

Salt and pepper, to taste

2 tablespoons gluten-free Worcestershire sauce

2 small cloves garlic, crushed

2 teaspoons olive oil

12 fresh mushrooms, washed and stemmed

2 tablespoons chopped parsley

Freshly ground black pepper, to taste

1. Lightly whisk the egg whites in a large bowl. Add the whole eggs and milk and whisk until combined. Season lightly with salt and pepper.

2. Combine the Worcestershire sauce, garlic, and olive oil. Brush the mushrooms lightly with the Worcestershire sauce mixture, then grill or broil on medium heat for 5–7 minutes or until soft. Remove and keep warm.

3. Heat a nonstick frying pan and add the egg mixture, scraping the bottom gently with a flat plastic spatula to cook evenly. Cook until the egg is just set.

4. To serve, divide the scrambled eggs and mushrooms among 4 serving plates. Sprinkle the eggs with the chopped parsley and pepper. Serve immediately.

Spinach Omelet

The harmony of spinach and eggs makes this omelet not only pretty to look at but tasty and pleasing even to children.

SERVES 6
· · · · · · · · · ·

1 (10-ounce) package frozen chopped spinach, thawed and undrained

3 tablespoons gluten-free chicken broth

1 clove garlic, crushed

1/8 to 1/4 teaspoon pepper

1/4 cup Parmesan cheese or nondairy alternative such as blanched almond flour

10 eggs

2 tablespoons water

2 teaspoons butter or coconut oil divided

1. Combine spinach, broth, garlic, and pepper in a small saucepan; cover and simmer 20 minutes. Stir in Parmesan cheese; cook 1 minute or until cheese is melted, stirring constantly. (If using almond flour, sprinkle on each serving right before serving instead.) Set aside.

2. In a large bowl, combine eggs and water; beat lightly. Coat a 10" omelet pan or heavy skillet with 1 teaspoon butter. Place pan over medium heat until just hot enough to sizzle a drop of water.

3. Pour half of egg mixture into pan. As mixture starts to cook, gently lift edges of omelet with a spatula and tilt pan so uncooked portion flows underneath.

4. As mixture begins to set, spread half the spinach mixture over half the omelet. Loosen omelet with a spatula; fold in half and slide onto a warm serving platter.

5. Repeat procedure with remaining ingredients.

Veggie Omelet

Colorful veggies add to the crunch and the appeal of this easy-to-prepare omelet. Not only are they gluten-free ingredients, but they will also improve your family's overall health.

SERVES 2
....

½ cup thinly sliced mushrooms

¼ cup chopped green pepper

¼ cup chopped onion

1 tablespoon diced pimiento

3 eggs, yolks and whites separated

2 tablespoons mayonnaise

¼ teaspoon salt

⅛ teaspoon pepper

1. Combine mushrooms, green pepper, onion, and pimiento in a 1-quart casserole; cover loosely with heavy-duty plastic wrap and microwave on high for 3–3½ minutes or until vegetables are tender. Drain and set aside.

2. In a large bowl, beat egg whites until stiff peaks form. Combine egg yolks, mayonnaise, salt, and pepper; beat well. Gently fold egg whites into egg yolk mixture.

3. Coat a 9" glass pie plate or quiche pan with ½ teaspoon oil. Pour egg mixture into pie plate, spreading evenly. Microwave at medium (50 percent power) for 8–10½ minutes or until center is almost set, giving pie plate a half-turn after 5 minutes.

4. Spread vegetable mixture over half of omelet. Loosen omelet with spatula and fold in half. Slide the omelet onto a warm serving platter.

Veggies and Gluten

You will be delighted to know that all fresh veggies and fruits are totally gluten free in their natural state. Grow your own, pick your own, or buy them fresh from the market—it doesn't matter as long as you cook with the freshest fruits and vegetables possible.

Breakfast Potatoes

Potatoes are great for breakfast and these will wake up your taste buds. These easy potatoes, which are made quickly in the microwave, are the perfect solution for a school-day breakfast!

SERVES 2
• • • • • • • • • •

1 large baking potato

1½ tablespoons butter or coconut oil

¼ teaspoon celery salt

¼ teaspoon paprika

⅛ teaspoon pepper

¼ cup finely chopped fresh parsley

1. Scrub potato and pat dry. Prick several times with a fork. Place potato on paper towel in microwave oven. Microwave on high 5–6 minutes, turning potato after 3 minutes.

2. Let potato stand 5 minutes to cool before checking for doneness. Cut potato into ¾" cubes and set aside.

3. Place butter in a 1½-quart casserole. Microwave 30 seconds or until melted.

4. Stir celery salt, paprika, and pepper into butter. Add potatoes and parsley. Toss all together.

5. Cover with casserole lid. Microwave on high for 2 minutes. Stir before serving. Serve with scrambled eggs and fresh fruit for a complete meal.

Make Scrambled Eggs in the Microwave!

In a small bowl whisk together 2 large eggs. Whisk in 1–2 tablespoons of milk or almond milk, and ⅛ teaspoon each of salt and pepper. In a small microwaveable casserole dish, place 2 teaspoons of butter or coconut oil. Melt butter for 10 seconds until melted. Pour in whisked eggs and cook for 20–30 seconds at a time, stirring in between, until the scrambled eggs are the cooked consistency you prefer.

CHAPTER 4

SENSATIONAL SALADS AND SLAWS

Avocado Summer Salad

This recipe works nicely with many different summer fruits. Experiment with a variety of berries to provide different sources of vitamins, minerals, and antioxidants.

MAKES 5 CUPS (4 SERVINGS)

2 ripe avocados

2 fresh nectarines

¾ cup strawberries, diced

¼ cup sweet onion, diced

3 tablespoons fresh-squeezed lime juice

Salt and freshly ground black pepper, to taste

1. Remove the pit from the avocados and slice into long strips. Pit and dice the nectarines.

2. Mix together the nectarines, strawberries, and onion in a bowl. Toss the mixture until evenly coated.

3. Arrange the avocado slices on a plate. Squeeze lime juice over the avocados to help maintain freshness.

4. Top avocados with the mixture of nectarines, strawberries, and onions. Season with salt and pepper.

Chicken Salad

Use this to stuff pea pods or celery as a fun snack for your children. You can also wrap it in a warmed corn tortilla for a sandwich.

MAKES 10 OUNCES (4 SERVINGS)

10 ounces canned white meat chicken, drained

¼ cup dried blueberries or chopped apples

¼ cup mayonnaise

Combine all ingredients in a medium bowl.

Citrus Fruit Salad

Pair this recipe with the Cinnamon Yogurt Fruit Dip found in Chapter 11. These two dishes together provide great sources of vitamin C and calcium. Jicama also provides a source of folic acid in this dish!

MAKES 4 SERVINGS

2 oranges, peeled and sliced

1 cup pineapple, sliced

½ cup jicama, cut into matchsticks

1 cup blueberries

½ cup shredded coconut

1. In a medium bowl combine the orange, pineapple, and jicama slices with the blueberries.

2. Top with shredded coconut to taste.

Citrusy Rice Salad

Keep the extra dressing in a separate container to re-dress any leftover salad.

MAKES 3 CUPS (6 SERVINGS)

¼ cup fresh green beans (or ¼ cup
  cooked green beans, skipping step 1)

¼ cup chopped orange pieces

¼ cup pineapple chunks

2 scallions

2 cups cooked short-grain brown rice

¼ cup orange juice

1 teaspoon sugar

¼ cup olive oil

1. Steam green beans until tender. Plunge into cold water to stop cooking process.

2. Cut fruit and beans into bite-size pieces. Thinly slice white portion of scallions.

3. In a large bowl, combine rice, fruit, and vegetables.

4. In a jar with a tight-fitting lid, combine orange juice, sugar, and olive oil. Shake to combine.

5. Toss salad with dressing to taste.

Cucumber Tomato Salad

This versatile salad can act as a dip for corn chips, or it can be used as a topping for fish or chicken.

MAKES 4 CUPS
. . . .

4 tomatoes

1 cucumber

½ red onion

1 tablespoon minced garlic

2 tablespoons extra-virgin olive oil

3 tablespoons gluten-free red wine vinegar

Salt and pepper, to taste

1. Dice tomatoes, cucumber, and onion.

2. In large mixing bowl, add all the ingredients. Toss to combine. For best flavor chill salad for 2 hours or more before serving. Store any leftovers in an airtight container in the refrigerator for up to 1 week.

Picking an Olive Oil Is Confusing!

There are four descriptors that show the degree of processing in the olive oil. Extra-virgin olive oil means that this is the oil from the first pressing of the olives. Virgin olive oil is from the second pressing. Pure olive oil is then refined and filtered slightly. Extra-light oil has been highly refined and retains only a mild olive flavor. For most of the baking recipes that call for oil in this cookbook, use light-tasting olive oil, which is not lighter in calories, but doesn't have the strong taste of olives (as the extra-virgin olive oil does). It's an extremely healthy, non–genetically modified (as opposed to canola oil, corn oil, or soy oil), omega-3 fatty acid–rich oil.

Fruit Salad

Added sweeteners and/or a dressing isn't necessary when you mix together this colorful, fresh, and flavorful fruit salad.

MAKES 3 CUPS

½ cup honeydew cubes

½ cup cantaloupe cubes

½ cup seedless watermelon cubes

½ cup blueberries

½ cup pineapple cubes

½ cup strawberry slices

In a large bowl, add all ingredients. Toss to combine.

An Old-Fashioned Watermelon Basket

To make a fun presentation for fruit salad, cut a watermelon in half, and scoop out the pink flesh, leaving behind the green-and-white shell. Cut up the watermelon and other fruits, combine, and use the watermelon shell as your serving bowl.

Tabbouleh Salad

This version of the perfect summer salad is made with quinoa instead of couscous to create a healthy gluten-free meal. Make this salad at the peak of tomato season to use some of the best-tasting tomatoes produced all year!

MAKES 8 CUPS (6 SERVINGS)

3 cups quinoa, cooked

1 cup cannellini beans

1½ cups parsley, finely chopped

3 large tomatoes, chopped

3 green onions, sliced

1 tablespoon mint, finely chopped

¼ cup extra-virgin olive oil

¼ cup lemon juice

1. In a large bowl, combine all ingredients.
2. Chill for 2–3 hours and then serve.

Green Salad with Homemade Egg-Free Caesar Dressing

Add Fresh Croutons from Chapter 11 for a crunchy and delicious topping.

MAKES 8 CUPS

1 head of romaine lettuce, washed and torn

2 tomatoes, cut into wedges

2 garlic cloves

2 tablespoons Dijon mustard

1 tablespoon anchovy paste

¼ cup–⅓ cup extra virgin olive oil

½ cup lemon juice

1 tablespoon Worcestershire sauce

1 teaspoon freshly ground black pepper

1. Combine lettuce and tomatoes in large mixing bowl.

2. In a blender, combine remainder of ingredients and blend until smooth for dressing.

3. Toss salad with desired amount of dressing. Store any leftover dressing in sealed glass jar in the refrigerator for up to 1 week.

Trying to Cut Back on Oil? Use White Beans Instead

If you prefer to use less oil in this recipe, simply use ⅓ cup cooked white beans + 2 tablespoons olive oil when emulsifying the dressing. It will make a creamy, white dressing. You may need to add additional lemon juice or water to thin the dressing out, if necessary.

Lemony Rice and Asparagus Salad

Save extra dressing for leftover rice salad. Overnight, the rice will absorb the dressing and will benefit from the extra flavor.

MAKES 4 CUPS (8 SERVINGS)

2 cups enriched white rice

4 cups water

1 bunch asparagus

¼ cup olive oil

½ cup lemon juice

2 tablespoons fresh dill, minced

1. In a medium saucepan, bring rice and water to a boil.
2. Reduce heat, cover, and simmer 20 minutes, or until liquid is absorbed. Let rice sit covered 5 minutes before fluffing with a fork.
3. While rice cooks, clean asparagus and remove tough ends. Chop asparagus into 1" pieces. Steam asparagus until bright and tender.
4. In a lidded jar, combine olive oil and lemon juice. Shake to combine.
5. In a large bowl, combine rice, asparagus, dill, and ½ cup of the dressing. Chill for 1–2 hours before serving. Store any leftover salad in an airtight container in the refrigerator for up to 1 week.

Asparagus, the Plant That Keeps on Giving

Asparagus is a perennial plant; it is a member of the lily family. Asparagus spears are the shoots that grow from a crown that is planted approximately 3 feet underground. Although the shoots or spears are not picked for the first three years, the same plant can produce spears for fifteen to twenty years.

Mango Coleslaw

The collard greens and coleslaw can be cooked for this recipe if your child doesn't like the crunchy texture of the raw vegetables.

MAKES 8 CUPS (6 SERVINGS)

3 stalks of collard greens

5 cups coleslaw prepared mix

3 ripe mangos or 3 cups frozen mango

¼ cup red onion, chopped

2 tablespoons olive oil

1 tablespoon gluten-free balsamic vinegar

1 tablespoon light sugar or honey

1. Chop collard greens into tiny pieces.

2. In large mixing bowl, combine coleslaw mixture, collard greens, mango, and onion.

3. In small mixing bowl, combine olive oil, vinegar, and sugar and mix well to create dressing.

4. Pour dressing over contents in large mixing bowl. Toss and serve. Store any leftover salad in an airtight container in the refrigerator for up to 1 week.

Why Are Collard Greens So Good for You?

Collard greens are excellent sources of vitamins K, A, and C. Furthermore, they are a good source of the nutrient manganese. What is manganese? It helps your body to be able to use the vitamin C that is in your diet. Manganese is also vital in the chemical processes that help create natural antioxidants in your body.

Quinoa and Bean Salad

The key to successful quinoa is to thoroughly rinse your quinoa before you cook it. Rinsing the quinoa removes the thin, outer coating on each seed that tastes quite bitter.

MAKES 6 CUPS (6 SERVINGS)

1 cup rinsed quinoa

2 cups water

1 (15-ounce) can kidney beans

1 cup frozen corn

1 red pepper, finely chopped

Juice of 1 lemon

⅓ cup cilantro, finely chopped

3 tablespoons gluten-free balsamic vinegar

½ cup olive oil

2 tablespoons cumin

Salt, to taste

1. Rinse the quinoa under cold running water until the water runs clear.

2. In a medium saucepan, place quinoa and water. Set over medium heat and cook 10–15 minutes or until all the water is absorbed. Fluff with fork.

3. Combine quinoa with remaining ingredients. Mix thoroughly, chill, and serve. Store any leftovers in an airtight container in the refrigerator for up to 1 week.

Quinoa Is a Healthy Vegetarian Protein

Quinoa (pronounced 'keen-wah') is an ancient plant (that may have originated in Peru) which has edible seeds. The plant has been cultivated for centuries as a food source in South America. The seed is unique because it contains a large amount of healthy vegetable protein, fiber, and many vitamins and minerals such as iron, magnesium, vitamin E, and potassium.

Roasted Potato Salad

Roasting potatoes adds some variety to the traditional boiled potatoes that are usually used in potato salads. Roasting is an easy process that adds a nice surprising flavor to your potato salad.

MAKES 4 CUPS

2 pounds new potatoes

4 tablespoons gluten-free Italian dressing

½ red onion, chopped

¼ cup Parmesan cheese (optional)

½ teaspoon sea salt

¼ teaspoon pepper

1. Cut raw potatoes into bite-size pieces and toss with dressing.

2. Arrange potatoes on a baking sheet and put into cold oven.

3. Heat oven to 450°F and roast potatoes for 20–30 minutes. Turn potatoes over about halfway through the roasting process to allow even roasting.

4. Remove from oven, allow to cool, and toss with remaining ingredients in a large bowl. Store any leftovers in an airtight container in the refrigerator for up to 1 week.

Easy Pasta Salad

Serve this cool, summery salad stuffed into a tomato or melon half. You can also serve it over shredded lettuce and tomatoes.

MAKES 3 CUPS (6 SERVINGS)

½ cup mayonnaise

2 tablespoons yellow mustard

¼ minced sweet onion, like Vidalia

½ cup shredded carrot

½ teaspoon dried dill

4 cups cooked gluten-free macaroni pasta, such as Heartland Pasta

1. In a large bowl, whisk together mayonnaise, mustard, sweet onion, carrot, and dill.

2. Fold in pasta and stir to coat. Refrigerate for 2–3 hours before serving for best flavor. Store any leftovers in an airtight container in the refrigerator for up to 3 days.

Perfect Gluten-Free Pasta

Gluten-free pasta can easily be overcooked and become mushy, especially after being refrigerated overnight. Some people do not like the taste or texture of brown rice pasta, and prefer gluten-free pasta made from corn or quinoa, both of which tend to hold up better to refrigeration. To cook gluten-free pasta, pour dry pasta into a large pot of boiling, well-salted water. Cook the pasta for 8–10 minutes until it is "al dente," or still has some bite to it. For a cold salad like this one, strain the pasta and run thoroughly cold water over it to end cooking immediately. For a hot pasta dish, strain the pasta, quickly run it through cold water and then drizzle a small amount of olive oil over the pasta to keep it from sticking. Add to sauce and serve.

Sweet Potato Salad

Combining sweet potatoes and russet potatoes is a nice twist to a familiar dish.

MAKES 8 SERVINGS

4 russet potatoes

2 sweet potatoes

3 eggs

3 tablespoons sweet pickle relish

¼ cup finely chopped celery

2 scallion onions, chopped

½ cup mayonnaise

1 tablespoon yellow mustard

Sea salt and pepper, to taste

1. In a large saucepan, boil water for potatoes and boil until soft. Once soft, remove from heat and cut potatoes into bite-size pieces.

2. In small pot, cover eggs with cold water and bring to boil. Cover and remove from heat for approximately 10 minutes. Remove from water, cool, peel, and chop.

3. Place eggs and potatoes in large mixing bowl.

4. Add sweet pickle relish, chopped celery, scallions, mayonnaise, and mustard, and mix thoroughly.

5. Salt and pepper to taste. Refrigerate until served. Store any leftovers in an airtight container in the refrigerator for up to 1 week.

Are Sweet Potatoes Really Potatoes?

No! There are more than 100 varieties of edible potatoes but the sweet potato is not one of them! These two root vegetables are completely different! The potato's scientific name is *Solanum tuberosum*, and its relatives are tomatoes, eggplants, and peppers. The sweet potato's scientific name is *Ipomoea batatas*, and it is in another plant family. Sweet potatoes are more closely related to morning glories than they are to regular potatoes!

Black Bean Slaw

And you thought coleslaw was just shredded cabbage! There are hundreds of different kinds of cabbage, and adding different ingredients and dressings gives you a wide variety of tasty options!

SERVES 8

2½ cups finely shredded cabbage

1 (15-ounce) can black beans, rinsed and drained

½ cup shredded carrot

½ cup chopped purple onion

¼ cup chopped fresh cilantro

½ cup plain yogurt or nondairy alternative such as So Delicious Coconut Milk Yogurt

½ cup salsa

2 tablespoons mayonnaise

2 teaspoons white wine vinegar

2 teaspoons lime juice

Fresh cilantro sprigs (optional)

1. In a large bowl, combine cabbage, beans, carrot, onion, and chopped cilantro. Toss well.

2. In a small bowl, combine yogurt, salsa, mayonnaise, vinegar, and lime juice. Stir well. Pour over cabbage mixture and gently toss.

3. Tightly cover. Refrigerate at least 2 hours. Garnish with fresh cilantro sprigs if desired.

Veggie Slaw

A dish with fresh red cabbage always makes a pretty addition to a table setting, and it's a double win when it tastes great too!

SERVES 4

1½ cups shredded red cabbage

1 cup shredded carrot

¾ cup shredded yellow squash

¾ cup shredded zucchini

½ cup chopped green pepper

⅓ cup finely chopped onion

¼ cup unsweetened pineapple juice

1½ tablespoons sugar

3 tablespoons cider vinegar

2 tablespoons water

¼ teaspoon paprika

¼ teaspoon celery seeds

⅛ teaspoon garlic powder

Dash of ground red pepper

1. In a large bowl, combine cabbage, carrot, yellow squash, zucchini, green pepper, and chopped onion.

2. In a small bowl, combine pineapple juice, sugar, vinegar, water, paprika, celery seeds, garlic powder, and red pepper. Stir well.

3. Pour dressing over vegetable mixture. Toss gently.

4. Cover tightly and refrigerate at least 4 hours before serving. Toss gently at serving time.

Red Cabbage Trivia

Some people call red cabbage by a slightly different name—purple cabbage. Its color does change according to the environment it's in; it will even turn blue if served with nonacidic food. All colors aside, red cabbage happens to be much higher in vitamin C than other types of cabbage.

Wild Rice Cranberry Salad

Ruby-red cranberries and fresh green onions lend a vibrant, festive addition to your dinner table. This salad can be served chilled or at room temperature.

SERVES 4

6 ounces wild rice, uncooked

6 ounces fresh cranberries

¼ cup cranberry juice cocktail

1 tablespoon sugar

½ cup carrots cut in strips

1 cup minced green onions

1 tablespoon apple cider vinegar

2 teaspoons olive oil or sesame oil

Dash freshly ground black pepper

1. Prepare rice according to package directions. Set aside.

2. In a medium saucepan, combine cranberries, juice, and sugar. Cook over medium heat. Stir occasionally until cranberries pop, about 5 minutes. Remove from heat and cool slightly.

3. Transfer cranberry mixture to a large mixing bowl. Add remaining ingredients. Toss gently until combined well.

4. Cover and refrigerate until serving time. Store any leftovers in an airtight container in the refrigerator for up to 1 week.

CHAPTER 5

SOUP'S ON!

Basic Chicken Noodle Soup

Gluten-free noodles are available in a variety of shapes. For this soup, choose a smaller-size variety. To save a step in this recipe, make the soup as directed, except leave out the cooked noodles. When ready to serve, simply place ⅓ cup cooked noodles into each bowl. This is especially helpful as gluten-free noodles tend to get soggy if left in hot broth for a long period of time.

MAKES 8 CUPS

Approximately 10 cups water (enough to cover chicken)

1 large broiler-fryer chicken

3–4 celery stalks, chopped

4–6 carrots, chopped

1 large onion

Salt and pepper, to taste

2 bay leaves

2 teaspoons gluten-free chicken bouillon, such as Better than Bouillon Organic Chicken Base

1½ cups cooked gluten-free noodles (small size)

1. Bring water to a boil in a large stock pot. Add chicken and return to a boil.

2. Once boiling, reduce heat immediately. Skim top of soup with a handheld metal or plastic strainer.

3. Add remaining ingredients and simmer for 1½ hours.

4. Remove chicken and set aside. Remove all vegetables and discard bay leaf.

5. Strain soup and allow to cool. Skim off hardened fat.

6. Reheat soup on low heat and add cooked noodles. Serve once soup has heated through.

Flavorful Variations

The beauty of this basic soup is that you can easily add your favorite flavors and in-season vegetables. Do you have lots of fresh summer tomatoes and zucchini? Roughly chop 2 of each and add them into the soup an hour before serving. Do you love fresh herbs like basil and thyme? Add them in the last 30 minutes of cooking.

Lentil Soup

Divide leftovers of this soup and freeze in small portions to have a quick healthy weekday lunch. Allow your kids to help by looking through the lentils to remove any bad ones and then let them rinse the beans with cold water through a metal strainer.

MAKES 6 CUPS

1 tablespoon olive oil

1 clove garlic

¾ cup diced onion

4 cups water

1 gluten-free bouillon cube (vegetable, chicken, or beef)

1 cup diced carrots

½ cup diced celery

½ cup lentils

2 cups diced tomatoes with liquid

1. In a large stock pot, heat olive oil over medium-high flame. Add the garlic and onion and sauté for 5 minutes.

2. Add water, bouillon cube, carrots, and celery.

3. Rinse and pick over lentils, and add to pot.

4. Add tomatoes.

5. Cover the pot and simmer for 45 minutes. Serve.

A Soup a Day . . .

Soups are a fantastic base for children's menus. It is easy to incorporate many different vegetables in soups that your child may not venture to taste on his or her own.

Taco Soup

This is a great meal on a cold night! It is a chili with a taco twist. Serve this with some baked or fried corn tortilla strips on top for a nice crunch to the soup.

MAKES 8 CUPS

2 pounds lean ground beef, ground turkey, or shredded chicken

1 teaspoon olive oil

1 large onion, diced

2 (14-ounce) cans diced tomatoes with chilis, not drained

1 (14-ounce) can red kidney beans, not drained

1 (10-ounce) bag of frozen corn

1 Taco Seasoning Mixture (see Chapter 6) OR 1 (1.25-ounce) package gluten-free taco seasoning mix such as McCormicks

1. In a large sauté pan, brown beef or turkey and drain. If you are using chicken, boil the chicken until cooked, remove from water, and shred.

2. In a large stock pot, heat olive oil over medium-high flame. Add onion and sauté for 5 minutes, until clear.

3. Add meat, tomatoes, kidney beans, frozen corn, and Taco Seasoning Mixture. Mix together well.

4. Heat over medium heat until heated through about 20–30 minutes.

Chicken and Vegetable Soup

When chicken is slowly simmered in broth it becomes soft and is very easy to chew, which makes it an incredibly healthy and hearty meal for young children.

MAKES 8 CUPS
....

1 pound boneless chicken breasts cut into ¼" pieces

½ red onion, diced

2 celery ribs, sliced

1 medium carrot, sliced

¼ red bell pepper, diced

3 cloves garlic, minced

2 tablespoons butter

2 tablespoons olive oil

1 teaspoon dried basil

½ teaspoon dried oregano

⅛ teaspoon pepper

3 (14½-ounce) cans gluten-free chicken broth

1 (14½-ounce) can diced tomatoes, undrained

½ summer squash or zucchini, sliced

4 cups gluten-free rotini, cooked according to package directions

5 ounces fresh spinach, chopped

1. In a large saucepan, sauté the chicken, onion, celery, carrots, red pepper, and garlic in butter and oil for 5 minutes.

2. Stir in the basil, oregano, and pepper until blended.

3. Slowly add chicken broth, tomatoes, and squash.

4. Bring to a boil. Reduce heat; cover and simmer for 1 hour.

5. Return to a boil; stir in the pasta and spinach.

6. Reduce heat; simmer, uncovered, for 5–10 minutes or until spinach is tender.

Cream of Potato Soup

Slow cookers can be an easy way to prepare meals for your family. Assemble the ingredients in the morning and then forget about it until it's time for dinner!

MAKES 6 SERVINGS

6 potatoes, peeled and cubed

2 onions, chopped

1 carrot, sliced

1 stalk celery, sliced

4 gluten-free bouillon cubes (vegetable, chicken, or beef)

1 tablespoon dried parsley flakes

5 cups water

⅓ cup butter or olive oil

1½ cups milk or unsweetened almond milk

1. Put all ingredients except milk into a slow cooker.

2. Cover and cook on low for 10–12 hours or on high for 3–4 hours.

3. Stir in milk in last hour of cooking. If the soup isn't as thick as you would like, add instant gluten-free mashed potatoes flakes, 2 tablespoons at a time, until the soup is as thick as you'd like it.

Sweetened vs. Unsweetened Almond Milk

This book calls for both unsweetened almond milk and "regular" almond milk. Here's why: You will often find "original" almond milk to contain not only a sweetener (usually sugar), but also vanilla flavoring. This variety works great in baked goods and adds additional flavor and moisture, but for savory applications such as soups or casseroles, you'll want to use unsweetened almond milk, which will mimic regular "dairy" milk more closely and not contain extra sugar.

Creamy Cauliflower Soup

For added texture, remove ⅓ of the soup before puréeing. After soup is puréed, return to pot and combine with reserved soup. Nutritional yeast is a deactivated yeast that is popular among vegans and those who cannot tolerate dairy products. It adds a "cheesy," savory flavor to main dishes and is delicious in this soup. However, if you cannot find it in your area, feel free to leave it out of this recipe.

MAKES 6 CUPS

½ onion, diced

1 tablespoon olive oil

3 medium potatoes, peeled and diced

1 medium cauliflower, chopped

4 cups gluten-free vegetable broth

2 tablespoons nutritional yeast, optional

½ teaspoon white pepper

½ teaspoon sea salt

1 bay leaf

1 cup plain yogurt or nondairy alternative such as coconut milk

1. In a large stock pot, sauté onion in olive oil for 5 minutes.

2. Add remaining ingredients, bring to a boil.

3. Reduce heat to a simmer. Simmer approximately 30 minutes until potatoes and cauliflower are tender.

4. Remove bay leaf.

5. Purée soup in blender until smooth.

The White "Green" Vegetable

The saying "eat your green vegetables" should have the amendment—"and cauliflower." This late-season nutritional powerhouse is a cruciferous vegetable; it's in the same family as broccoli, cabbage, and kale. It has high levels of vitamin C and significant amounts of vitamin B6, folate, and dietary fiber.

Minestrone Soup

This hearty, delicious soup is great for a crowd! Use this for winter gatherings or potluck dinners. Rice stands in for pasta in this healthy dish.

MAKES 10 CUPS

1 red onion, chopped

3 cloves garlic, minced

1 tablespoon olive oil

6 cups gluten-free stock (vegetable, chicken, or beef)

2 (14½-ounce) cans stewed tomatoes with Italian seasoning

1 large potato, cubed

2 stalks celery, chopped

2 carrots, chopped

¼ large head cabbage, finely chopped

1 cup uncooked brown rice

½ tablespoon thyme

½ tablespoon oregano

2 tablespoons chopped fresh basil

1 (15-ounce) can cannellini beans

2 cups fresh corn kernels

1 large zucchini, sliced

¼ cup parsley, chopped

Salt and pepper, to taste

Parmesan cheese, or nondairy alternative such as blanched almond flour, optional

1. In a large soup pot, sauté onions and garlic in 1 tablespoon olive oil until clear, about 5–7 minutes.

2. Add in the stock, undrained tomatoes, potato, celery, carrot, cabbage, rice, thyme, oregano, and basil.

3. Bring to a boil and reduce heat. Simmer for about 15 minutes.

4. Stir in the beans, corn, zucchini, and parsley.

5. Simmer for 20–30 more minutes until the vegetables are tender.

6. Season with salt and pepper. Sprinkle with Parmesan cheese to serve.

Beaneaters!

Cannellini beans are so popular in the Tuscany region in Italy that the Tuscan people have been nicknamed *mangiafagiole*, which means beaneaters. These beans can be used in place of great northern beans or navy beans in most recipes. The nutritional benefits are that they are high in fiber, folate, iron, and magnesium.

Split Pea Soup

This protein-rich soup is also a good source of vitamin A, vitamin C, potassium, and dietary fiber.

MAKES 6 CUPS

1 cup split peas

1 medium onion

1 medium carrot

1 medium baking potato

1 teaspoon olive oil

3 cups gluten-free broth (vegetable, chicken, or beef)

¼ teaspoon dried summer savory

⅛ teaspoon cumin

1 bay leaf

1. Pick over split peas and remove any debris. Rinse, drain, and set aside.

2. Finely chop onion, carrot, and potato.

3. In a stock pot, heat olive oil over medium-high heat. Add vegetables and sauté until soft, approximately 3 minutes.

4. Add remaining ingredients. Stir. Simmer uncovered 40 minutes, or until split peas are very soft.

5. Remove bay leaf.

6. Add more broth for a thinner soup, if desired.

Different Tastes

Culture largely dictates what foods "go together." Your child might think that other combinations are more appealing. For example, try adding chopped fruit to mashed sweet potatoes for a vitamin-rich comfort food or serving cooled Split Pea Soup as a dip for gluten-free corn chips or potato chips.

Creamy Corn Chowder

For a smooth soup, blend all of it, rather than reserving some to mix in.

MAKES 7 CUPS

4 baking potatoes

1 onion

2 large, peeled carrots

1 green bell pepper

4 cups fresh sweet corn (or 1 pound frozen)

6 cups water

2 gluten-free bouillon cubes (vegetable, chicken, or beef)

1 cup milk or nondairy alternative, such as unsweetened almond milk

Freshly ground black pepper, to taste

1. Coarsely chop all vegetables, except corn.
2. Combine all ingredients, except milk and pepper, in a large stock pot. Bring to a boil.
3. Reduce heat; simmer ½ hour or until vegetables are tender.
4. Remove 5 cups of soup from pot and blend until smooth in a blender. Return blended soup to pot.
5. Mix in milk and pepper to taste; heat before serving.

Turkey Chili

If this chili is not spicy enough for the adults, add extra chili powder and green chilis or serrano peppers to an adult portion and heat through.

MAKES 12 CUPS

2 tablespoons olive oil

1 red onion, chopped

1 clove garlic, minced

1 pound ground turkey breast

1 pound butternut squash, peeled, seeded and cut into 1" cubes

½ cup gluten-free chicken broth

2 (14½-ounce) cans petite diced tomatoes

1 (15-ounce) can black beans with liquid

1 (15½-ounce) can white hominy, drained

1 (8-ounce) can tomato sauce

2 teaspoons chili powder

1 tablespoon ground cumin

⅛ teaspoon cinnamon

8 ounces plain yogurt or plain nondairy yogurt, optional

1. In a large pot, heat the oil over medium heat. Add onion and garlic; cook and stir for 3 minutes until clear.

2. Add turkey. Stir until crumbly and no longer pink.

3. Add the butternut squash, chicken broth, tomatoes, black beans, hominy, and tomato sauce; season with chili powder, cumin, and cinnamon.

4. Bring to a simmer, then reduce heat to medium-low, cover, and simmer until the squash is tender, about 20 minutes.

5. Top each bowl with 1–2 tablespoons of yogurt to serve.

Vegetable Rice Stew

The rice thickens this stew significantly, especially the longer it cooks. If you prefer a thinner stew, feel free to add an additional 1 or 2 cups of water to create more broth.

MAKES 10 CUPS
. . . .

1 carrot

1 celery stalk

1 potato

½ small onion

1 small sweet potato

1 cup chopped spinach

1 cup brown rice

8 cups water

1 (15-ounce) can diced tomatoes

½ teaspoon dried oregano

½ teaspoon dried basil

½ teaspoon dried thyme

1. Finely chop all vegetables.

2. Combine all ingredients in a large stock pot. Bring to a boil.

3. Reduce heat, cover, and simmer for 45 minutes or until rice is soft. Serve soup with gluten-free toast or crackers.

Flexible Foods

There is almost nothing as frustrating as starting a recipe, confident that you have all of the ingredients on hand, and then discovering that you're missing a key component of your dish. Not to worry, because there is often an easy substitute right in your own pantry. For example, if you don't have brown rice for this recipe, try substituting with white rice or quinoa in the same quantity. For dessert recipes, if you don't have strawberries, try blueberries or peaches instead. In other savory recipes different types of greens can often be substituted for each other, so if your recipe calls for spinach and you only have collards, go ahead and give it a try!

White Chili

This is an all-white chili, meaning all the ingredients that go into it are the color white. Try this as a way to excite your child about a meal; serve an "all-same-color" meal every once in a while. For instance, an orange meal might be orange slices, mashed sweet potatoes, and gluten-free macaroni and cheese with carrot coins.

MAKES 8 CUPS

1 medium onion, chopped

2 cloves garlic, minced

1 tablespoon olive oil

2 organic cooked chicken breasts, cubed

1 (12-ounce) can white corn, drained

1 (15-ounce) can cannellini beans, drained

1 (15-ounce) can garbanzo beans, drained

1 (4-ounce) can green chilis

2 (14½-ounce) cans gluten-free chicken broth

6 ounces shredded Monterey jack cheese or nondairy alternative such as Daiya Monterey Jack cheese

1. In large stock pot, sauté onion and garlic in oil until tender, about 5–7 minutes.

2. Add chicken breasts, white corn, cannellini beans, garbanzo beans, green chilis, and chicken broth to pot and simmer for 20–30 minutes or until heated through and beans are tender.

3. Top each serving with cheese.

Healthy Vegetable Broth Soup with Tomatoes and Spinach

Warm broth is a nourishing and comforting light meal for any season, especially when little ones are sick. Young children can easily digest this healing vegetarian meal. If you want to add more substance to the broth for a heartier meal, try adding ½ cup of cooked lentils or white beans.

MAKES 8 CUPS

3 tablespoons minced garlic

¼ teaspoon dried thyme

½ teaspoon paprika

2 tablespoons olive oil

6 cups gluten-free vegetable broth

1 bunch fresh spinach, cleaned and chopped

1½ cups diced tomato

Salt and pepper, to taste

1. Over medium heat, sauté garlic, thyme, and paprika in olive oil until the garlic is fragrant, but not browned.

2. In a large stock pot bring broth to a boil; add garlic mixture to the boil and reduce heat to simmer.

3. Add the spinach to a skillet over medium heat until it wilts.

4. Add spinach and diced tomatoes to simmering broth.

5. Add salt and pepper to taste.

Boost Your Flavor with Broth!

Next time you're cooking rice, quinoa, or gluten-free pasta, consider using broth as the liquid instead of water. You will get a more flavorful dish to serve either on its own or to use in a recipe.

CHAPTER 6

ENTICING ENTRÉES

Baja-Style Fish Tacos

For adult palates, try making this dish more spicy by increasing the amount of jalapeño peppers or the cayenne pepper. Allow older children to choose the amount of sauce they would like on their own tacos by placing the sauce in a plastic squeeze bottle and passing it around the table.

MAKES 8 TACOS

1 teaspoon olive oil

1 pound cod; cut into 2-ounce portions

Juice of 1 lime

¾ teaspoon sea salt, divided

½ cup sour cream

½ cup mayonnaise

Juice of 2 limes

½ fresh jalapeño pepper, deseeded, halved, and deribbed

½ teaspoon dried oregano

½ teaspoon dried dill weed

¼ teaspoon ground cumin

¼ teaspoon cayenne

8 gluten-free corn tortillas

½ medium head cabbage, finely shredded

½ medium head red cabbage, finely shredded

1. Lightly oil a shallow baking dish with 1 teaspoon oil. Arrange fish in dish.

2. Sprinkle fish with the juice of 1 lime and ½ teaspoon sea salt. Cover with foil and bake at 400°F for 10–15 minutes. Remove from oven.

3. In a blender, combine ¼ teaspoon sea salt, sour cream, mayonnaise, juice of 2 limes, jalapeño pepper, oregano, dill weed, cumin, and cayenne to form sauce for tacos.

4. Heat corn tortillas lightly in skillet on stove, top each with one portion of cooked fish, drizzle with sauce, and place handful of both types of finely shredded cabbage on top. Serve.

How Hot Is Your Pepper?

The hotness of peppers is measured by the Scoville scale, which was developed by Wilbur Scoville in 1912. The range goes from 0 Scoville units to 16,000,000 Scoville units. The bell pepper is a 0 and the habanero is a 200,000. The jalapeño in this recipe scores about 5,000.

BBQ Fish

Some of the most common and environmentally friendly fish are Alaskan wild salmon, white sea bass, U.S.-farmed tilapia, and U.S.-farmed catfish.

MAKES 4 FILLETS
. . . .
4 fillets Alaska longline cod
1 cup gluten-free barbecue sauce
12 slices onion

1. Preheat oven to 350°F. Lay out 4 pieces of foil or parchment paper, each large enough to wrap around one fillet.

2. On each piece of foil or parchment paper, spread out ¼ cup barbecue sauce and 3 slices of onion, then lay a fillet in the center.

3. Fold up foil or paper and bake for about 10–15 minutes. Serve with steamed broccoli and baked French fries.

Barbecue Meatloaf Muffins

The flaxseed meal is acting as an egg replacer in this recipe. Alternatively, if your child can tolerate eggs, feel free to use 1 large egg in place of the flaxseed meal and water.

MAKES 12 MUFFINS

1 tablespoon flaxseed meal

3 tablespoons water

1½ pounds lean ground beef

1 cup tomato juice

¾ cup rolled gluten-free oats

¼ cup chopped onion

2 cloves garlic, minced

2 tablespoons oregano

1½ cups gluten-free barbecue sauce

1. Preheat oven to 350°F. Mix flaxseed meal and water. Stir and allow to sit for 2–3 minutes.

2. In a large bowl, combine meat, tomato juice, rolled oats, onion, garlic, and oregano. Add flaxseed meal and water combination to this mixture and knead until well mixed.

3. Portion out into a regular-sized muffin tin. Top each muffin with 2 tablespoons barbecue sauce.

4. Bake until internal temperature of 160°F is reached. Serve meatloaf with mashed potatoes and a fresh green salad. Store any leftovers in an airtight container in the refrigerator for up to 3 days.

Flaxseed Meal Can Replace Eggs!

Flaxseed meal can be used to replace the egg that is traditionally used in meatloaf. Flax meal is a great vegetarian source of omega-3 essential fatty acids, vitamins B1, B2, and C, and beta carotene. Additionally, flaxseeds are a good source of zinc and iron, with trace amounts of calcium and potassium. Adding flaxseeds to recipes also provides a healthy dose of fiber, which is often lacking in the standard American diet.

Beef Brochettes

If you are using bamboo skewers, soak them in water for about 1 hour before using to help prevent burning or catching them on fire while grilling. A "brochette" (in culinary terms) is a food served on a skewer.

MAKES 7 SKEWERS

1 cup gluten-free steak sauce, such as Heinz Traditional Steak Sauce

¼ cup Italian dressing

¼ cup sugar or honey

1 clove garlic, minced

1 pound beef sirloin or sirloin steak

1 red bell pepper, cut into squares

1 green bell pepper, cut into squares

1 pineapple, cut into squares

1. In blender, combine the steak sauce, dressing, sugar, and garlic. Blend until smooth. Pour into glass baking dish.

2. Cut beef into cubes and place beef in the baking dish, cover, and marinade overnight.

3. The next day assemble your skewers, alternating meat, pepper, pineapple, and pepper on the skewer.

4. Grill until done. Remove from skewer before giving to children. Try serving beef brochettes with steamed brown rice and a fruit salad. Store any leftovers in an airtight container in the refrigerator for up to 3 days.

Skewer Tips

You can also soak the skewers in beef broth for 1 hour, which will provide more flavor while cooking. Or coat the skewer lightly with oil, which can withstand the high heat of the grill. Instead of putting meat and vegetables on the same skewer, separate onto 2 different skewers since they have different cooking times.

Broccolini with Meat and Rigatoni

The meat in this dish can easily be omitted if you would prefer to have a vegetarian main dish. If you can't find fresh broccolini in your local grocery store, try substituting regular broccoli or fresh asparagus.

MAKES 8 CUPS

1 pound gluten-free brown rice rigatoni pasta

4 tablespoons olive oil, divided

½ pound ground beef

1 tablespoon butter or coconut oil

4 cloves garlic, minced

1 bunch broccolini separated into florets

1 cup gluten-free broth (vegetable, chicken, or beef)

1 cup fresh basil, coarsely chopped, divided

Fresh parsley, chopped

Parmesan cheese or blanched almond flour (optional)

1. Cook rigatoni pasta according to directions, drain, drizzle lightly with about a tablespoon of olive oil, toss to coat, and set aside.

2. In medium pan, cook ground beef for 3–5 minutes over medium-high heat until browned. Drain and set aside.

3. In a large skillet, heat 3 tablespoons of olive oil and butter. Sauté garlic until browned over medium heat, about 1–2 minutes. Add broccolini and stir gently.

4. Add broth and simmer until broccolini is al dente, about 6–8 minutes.

5. Add half the basil, drained rigatoni, and ground beef to skillet and mix thoroughly.

6. Transfer to serving bowl, top with remaining basil, parsley, and Parmesan cheese. Store any leftovers in an airtight container in the refrigerator for up to 3 days.

Chicken and Broccoli Stir-Fry

If you are trying this recipe when broccoli is in season (usually in the fall) look for a fresh, local, organic variety in your grocery store. Want to be more creative? Use a mix of fresh vegetables such as cauliflower, water chestnuts, baby corn, and red peppers and make your own stir-fry mixture!

MAKES 8 CUPS
. . . .

1 pound boneless, skinless chicken breasts

2 cloves garlic, minced

3 tablespoons honey

1 tablespoon molasses or additional honey

2 tablespoons gluten-free soy sauce or soy-free Coconut Secret Coconut Aminos

2 tablespoons orange juice

½ teaspoon fresh ginger, grated

⅛ teaspoon sea salt

⅛ teaspoon freshly ground black pepper

1 package frozen broccoli stir-fry mix (broccoli, water chestnuts, peppers, corn)

2 teaspoons cornstarch

4 cups brown rice, cooked

1. Cut chicken into small strips.

2. Combine garlic, honey, molasses, soy sauce, orange juice, ginger, sea salt, and black pepper in a medium bowl. Add the chicken strips and marinate the chicken for 1 hour.

3. In a large, lightly oiled skillet, stir-fry chicken and marinade until chicken turns light brown and is done, about 8–10 minutes. Remove from skillet but keep warm.

4. In same skillet, stir-fry the vegetables until heated through and return chicken and marinade to pan.

5. In small bowl, combine cornstarch and cold water and mix until there are no lumps.

6. Place cornstarch in pan with chicken and vegetables. Allow this to come to a boil and cook for 1–2 minutes or until thickened.

7. Serve over brown rice. Store any leftovers in an airtight container in the refrigerator for up to 3 days.

The Origin of Stir-Frying!

Stir-frying developed during a period of time in China where cooking materials and food were in short supply. Items had to be cooked fast without wasting any food and with minimum fuel. Now, we know it is a healthful way to cook vegetables and preserve their nutrients.

Sweet & Sour Chicken over Rice Noodles

This chicken dish is vaguely reminiscent of pad thai, which has a balance of salty, sweet, sour, and spicy flavors all in one dish. If you prefer more heat, add additional garlic, ginger, and red pepper flakes.

MAKES 6 SERVINGS

1 pound boneless, skinless chicken breasts

2 (8-ounce) cans crushed pineapple in natural juices

9-ounce package of long rice noodles, such as fettuccine or rice pho noodles

¾ cup sunflower-seed butter or almond butter

½ cup light coconut milk

½ cup gluten-free vegetable or chicken broth

2½ ounces (1 small jar) carrot purée or carrot baby food

2 teaspoons garlic, minced

½ teaspoon ground ginger

2 tablespoons fresh lime juice

1–2 teaspoons sugar

⅛ teaspoon red pepper flakes (optional)

1. Preheat oven to 350°F.

2. Arrange chicken in 9" × 13" baking dish and pour in pineapple juice from crushed pineapple. Cover and bake until internal temperature reaches 170°F, about 15–20 minutes.

3. In large pot, boil about 8 cups of water. Once boiling, place rice noodles in water and boil until tender, approximately 8–10 minutes. Drain noodles and rinse with cold water.

4. While pasta is cooking, blend remaining ingredients in blender until smooth. Use extra broth to thin to desired consistency.

5. Return noodles to cooking pot and pour contents of blender onto noodles and stir.

6. Cut or shred chicken into age-appropriate-size pieces for your children; top with crushed pineapple. Serve with a side of the rice noodles with sunflower-seed butter sauce. Store any leftovers in an airtight container in the refrigerator for up to 3 days.

Easy Baked Chicken

The beautiful thing about chicken is it doesn't take a lot of ingredients to make a healthy, comforting, and delicious main dish. This is a very basic recipe for roasting chicken. Remember if you decide to use bone-in chicken pieces you will need to bake the chicken for 10–20 minutes longer than called for in this recipe.

SERVES 4–6

2 pounds boneless, skinless chicken breasts

4 tablespoons olive oil

½ teaspoon freshly ground black pepper

½ teaspoon sea salt

½ teaspoon garlic powder, optional

½ cup gluten-free chicken broth, optional

1. Preheat oven to 350°F.

2. Wash chicken and pat dry with a paper towel. Place chicken in a greased baking dish. Drizzle olive oil evenly over the chicken. Sprinkle chicken with ground black pepper and salt. Add garlic powder if desired.

3. Bake covered in aluminum foil for 15 minutes.

4. Remove foil and allow chicken to complete cooking uncovered, about 15–20 more minutes or until the juices run clear. The internal temperature of a cooked chicken breast should be 165°F. Serve chicken with steamed vegetables and a baked sweet potato on the side. Store any leftovers in an airtight container in the refrigerator for up to 3 days.

Baked Honey Pescado

This makes a very sweet fish. Children gobble it up, and adults may also enjoy it with the following modifications: no honey and 2½ tablespoons of Dijon mustard.

MAKES 4 SERVINGS

2 tablespoons wildflower honey

1½ tablespoons mustard

1½ tablespoons mayonnaise

1 teaspoon lemon juice

Sprinkle of sea salt

1 pound white sea bass

1. Preheat oven to 400°F.

2. In small bowl, combine honey, mustard, mayonnaise, lemon juice, and sea salt.

3. Place fish in a lightly oiled shallow baking dish. Spread honey mixture on top of fish.

4. Bake for 15 minutes or until fish flakes lightly with a fork. Serve with a fresh garden salad and gluten-free French bread, such as Gluten-Free Pantry's gluten-free French bread mix. Store any leftovers in an airtight container in the refrigerator for up to 3 days.

Looking for White Sea Bass in Your Local Store?

It often goes by a few different names such as king croaker, weakfish, or sea trout. This fish is typically caught in the wild off the Pacific Coast of the United States. It is a firm whitish fish that has a mild flavor. This is a good choice for seafood, as it is not overfished and is not at risk for high mercury contamination.

Horseradish Brisket

This is an excellent recipe for parties, holidays, or large gatherings. It is a large, crowd-pleasing dish! Serve this with Mashed Potatoes and Parsnips in Chapter 9 and the Green Salad with Homemade Egg-Free Caesar Dressing in Chapter 4.

SERVES 8–10

3–5 pounds beef brisket

1 (6-ounce) jar horseradish spread or 3 ounces fresh horseradish

1 (12-ounces) jar gluten-free barbecue sauce

1. Preheat oven to 250°F. Roll out a piece of foil to a size large enough to wrap around the whole brisket.

2. Place beef brisket in center of foil and cover with horseradish and barbecue sauce.

3. Fold up foil and bake for 5–6 hours, until done. Allow roast to rest for 10–15 minutes before slicing and serving. Store any leftovers in an airtight container in the refrigerator for up to 3 days or freeze for up to 3 months.

Chicken Corn Bites

These corn-coated chicken bites are a crunchy and fun addition to your child's menus! Bring a taste of the south to your table.

MAKES 16 BITES

½ cup light-tasting olive oil

2 cups cornmeal

¼ teaspoon hot paprika

½ teaspoon garlic salt

1 pound boneless, skinless chicken breasts, cut into strips

2 eggs, beaten

1. Heat oil in a medium skillet over high heat.

2. Process cornmeal in your blender until it is a fine flour, add paprika and garlic salt, and blend well. Place mixture in a zip-top bag.

3. Dip chicken strips in eggs, put in bag with cornmeal, and shake.

4. Fry chicken strips in oil until done, about 8–10 minutes; drain on paper towels and serve. These are best the day they are made; however, you can store any leftovers in an airtight container in the refrigerator for up to 3 days.

Farmer's Pie

This casserole is well suited for young diners, as it has a very tender consistency and a hint of sweetness thanks to the sweet potatoes.

MAKES A 3-QUART CASSEROLE (SERVES 6)

2 large sweet potatoes

1 tablespoon olive oil

2 cloves garlic, minced

¼ cup grated onion

¼ cup grated zucchini

¼ cup grated carrot

1 pound lean ground turkey or beef

½ cup plain yogurt or nondairy alternative such as So Delicious Coconut Milk Yogurt

½ teaspoon salt

3 tablespoons butter or coconut oil

1. Preheat oven to 350°F. Peel and dice sweet potatoes.

2. In a large saucepan, cover sweet potatoes with water and bring to a boil. Boil uncovered until tender, approximately 10 minutes.

3. While potatoes are cooking, heat olive oil in a medium skillet. Add garlic and vegetables. Sauté until soft, about 5 minutes.

4. Add ground turkey or beef continue to cook for 5–8 minutes until fully browned.

5. When sweet potatoes are tender, drain and return them to the pot. Mash the sweet potatoes with yogurt and salt using a potato masher or fork.

6. Pour the ground turkey or beef mixture into a greased 3-quart casserole dish. Spread the mashed sweet potatoes on top. Dot the top of the casserole with butter.

7. Bake uncovered for 40 minutes until top of casserole is golden brown. Serve with steamed green beans and a fruit salad.

Pork and Beans

Serve this on your favorite gluten-free rolls and top with a small amount of gluten-free barbecue sauce. Try this also as a side dish. Serve this pork and beans with fresh fruit salad or the Mango Coleslaw found in Chapter 4.

MAKES 6 CUPS (SERVES 6–8)

2 pounds boneless pork ribs

14 ounces gluten-free beef broth

1 (15-ounce) can black beans, drained

1 (12-ounce) bottle gluten-free mild barbecue sauce, divided

1. In slow cooker, place pork ribs and beef broth. Cook on high for 4 hours.

2. Once done, remove pork from cooker and shred pork.

3. In small saucepan, heat black beans until heated through.

4. Mix pork with 6 ounces barbecue sauce and black beans.

Rethink the Recipe

Pork and beans does not have to be chopped hot dogs and pinto beans! Adding spices and vegetables such as roasted red peppers, tomatoes, green peppers, and onions can also give your pulled pork a little kick. This pulled pork and bean mixture can also be wrapped in corn tortillas and topped with shredded cabbage to make a nice pork taco.

Shepherd's Pie

Be sure to check the labels on your Dijon mustard and Worcestershire sauce to ensure that they are gluten-free. The flaxseed in this recipe is completely optional, however it adds additional fiber and a nutty flavor to the meal.

MAKES 10 SERVINGS

3 large potatoes, peeled

1 tablespoon olive oil

1 red onion, chopped

½ cup diced carrots

1½ pounds ground beef

2 tablespoons flaxseed meal, optional

¾ cup gluten-free beef broth

¾ cup green peas

¾ cup corn

1 teaspoon gluten-free Worcestershire sauce, such as Lea & Perrins

1 teaspoon ketchup

1 teaspoon Dijon mustard

2 tablespoons butter or coconut oil

½ cup milk or nondairy alternative such as unsweetened almond milk

1. Preheat oven to 400°F.

2. In a large pot bring to a boil enough water to cover potatoes. Cut potatoes and place in boiling water.

3. In large skillet, heat 1 tablespoon olive oil. Sauté onions and carrots until tender. Add ground beef and flaxseed meal to pan and brown, about 10 minutes. Drain beef and return to hot skillet.

4. Add beef broth, peas, corn, Worcestershire sauce, ketchup, and Dijon mustard to skillet and heat for about 10 minutes.

5. Meanwhile, remove potatoes from boiling water when tender. Mash with butter and milk. Be careful not to make these potatoes too thin.

6. In a 9" × 13" pan, first layer and press meat mixture into the bottom of pan evenly. Then for the top layer, spread mashed potatoes on the top of meat mixture. Use a fork to arrange the potatoes into an even but pointy layer. There should be peaks of potatoes sticking up to get brown.

7. Bake for 30 minutes. Broil for 5 minutes at the end to crisp.

Taco Dinner

This recipe has very little heat, which makes it perfect for those children who don't like spicy food. To make it more spicy, pull your child's portion out of the skillet, then feel free to add hot sauce, peppers, and/or green chilies to the remaining meat.

MAKES 12 TACOS

1 pound lean ground beef or turkey

1 cup frozen corn, thawed

12 corn taco shells

2 cups shredded green cabbage

2 whole avocados, sliced

1 cup diced tomatoes

1. Preheat oven to 325°F.

2. In a medium skillet, brown ground beef and drain.

3. Return beef to skillet and add corn and heat.

4. Crisp up corn taco shells by placing them on a baking sheet in the oven at 300 degrees for about 5–7 minutes.

5. Add beef and corn mixture to taco shells and top with shredded cabbage, avocado slices, and tomatoes. Serve. If you have any leftover meat mixture, you can store it in an airtight container in the refrigerator for up to 3 days, or you can freeze it in a zip-top bag to save for future stews or soups.

Taco Seasoning Mixture

Make your own taco seasoning mixture! Mix the following: 1 tablespoon chili powder; ¼ teaspoon each of garlic powder, onion powder, crushed red pepper flakes, and dried oregano; ½ teaspoon each of cumin and paprika; and 1 teaspoon each of sea salt and black pepper.

Rotini with Bolognese Sauce

In Italy, bowls of pasta are layered differently than they are here in the United States. The sauce is the most important part of the meal, so the pasta is added to the sauce, instead of the sauce being added on top of the pasta!

MAKES 2 CUPS OF SAUCE (SERVES 8)

2 tablespoons olive oil

2 tablespoons butter or additional olive oil

½ sweet onion, diced

½ celery stalk, diced

½ carrot, diced

1 pound ground beef

15 ounces tomato sauce

2 tablespoons tomato paste

4 cups gluten-free rotini, cooked

Parmesan cheese or blanched almond flour (optional)

1. In a large pot, over medium heat, heat olive oil and butter. Add onion, celery, and carrots and sauté until onion is clear, about 3–5 minutes.

2. Add ground beef and cook thoroughly, about 8–10 minutes.

3. Add tomato sauce and paste and heat through.

4. Mix rotini and sauce, top with Parmesan cheese if using, and serve.

Want to Have Lunch in Rome?

In Italy, lunch is the largest meal of the day, often with many courses. Breakfast is typically very small, and dinner tends to be much smaller portions of leftovers from lunch. Italian diets are rich in whole grains, vegetables, fish, and olive oil. This type of "Mediterranean-style" diet is often associated with lower rates of heart disease.

Savory Rice and Sausage

This is so easy and really great for any time when you are really busy. Kids love it as much as grownups do! To lighten the fat content, use a turkey sausage.

SERVES 4–6

1 pound gluten-free Italian sausage, sweet or hot, cut into 1" pieces

1 medium onion, chopped fine

2 cloves garlic, chopped

1 cup uncooked white rice or brown rice

2¾ cups gluten-free chicken broth

1 teaspoon dried rosemary, or 1 tablespoon fresh rosemary

Parmesan cheese or blanched almond flour (optional)

Chopped fresh parsley, for garnish

1. In a large broiler-safe skillet over medium-high heat, brown the sausage pieces, onion, and garlic. If the sausage is very lean, add a bit of olive oil to prevent the food from sticking.

2. Stir in the rice and toss with the sausage and vegetables. Add the broth and rosemary and cover. Cook on very low heat or place in a 325°F oven for 45 minutes to 1 hour, depending on the type of rice you are using. (Do not use instant rice.)

3. Just before serving, sprinkle the top with Parmesan cheese and brown under the broiler. Add the chopped parsley and serve.

Crispy Potato-Crusted Chicken

When you use this crust on your baked chicken, you'll find it's really crispy and crunchy. Don't add salt as the potato chips are already salty.

SERVES 4

4 ounces potato chips

1 teaspoon freshly ground black pepper

2 tablespoons snipped fresh chives

1 teaspoon dried thyme

4 boneless, skinless chicken breasts

⅔ cup sour cream or mayonnaise

1. Preheat the oven to 350°F.

2. In a food processor, chop up potato chips until you have 1 cup of crumbs. In a small bowl, mix crumbs with the pepper, chives, and thyme.

3. Rinse the chicken, dry on paper towels, and lay it in a baking dish that you have prepared with nonstick spray.

4. Spread the chicken with sour cream, sprinkle with the potato chip crumb mixture, and bake for 25 minutes or until brown and crispy.

Alternatives to Bread Crumbs

Try using your food processor to make crumbs of such goodies as cornbread, potato chips, or popcorn. Check various rice cereals such as puffed rice and rice crisps to make sure they are gluten-free, then put them in your food processor to make crumbs. Store the crumbs in resealable plastic bags in the refrigerator.

The Best Roasted Turkey

For the sweetest, juiciest bird, try to find a turkey that is between 9 and 12 pounds. Make extra gravy by adding a can of chicken broth to the basting liquid.

SERVES 15

1 (10-pound) turkey

¼ cup olive oil

1 teaspoon dried thyme

½ cup fresh Italian flat-leaf parsley, rinsed and minced

Salt, to taste

1 teaspoon pepper

Giblets, including wing tips and neck

½ cup gluten-free chicken broth

2 bay leaves

4 strips bacon for bottom of roasting pan

2 teaspoons cornstarch

¼ cup water

1. Preheat the oven to 325°F. Rinse the turkey in cold water and pat dry.

2. In a small bowl, mix the olive oil, herbs, salt, and pepper thoroughly. Tease it under the skin of the breast, being careful not to tear the skin.

3. Place the giblets and wing tips in a saucepan with the broth and water to cover. Add the bay leaves. Cook for 2 hours, or while the turkey is cooking. Add extra water if the broth gets dry.

4. Put the bacon on the bottom of the roasting pan and place the turkey breast-side down on top of it. Place turkey in the oven. After 30 minutes, turn the turkey over. Arrange bacon over the breast and legs. Roast for 3 hours, basting every 20 minutes with the giblet stock and juices. Roast until the thickest part of the turkey breast is 165°F and the thigh is 175°F.

5. Make gravy by mixing 2 teaspoons cornstarch with ¼ cup water and blending with pan juices.

Roasting Turkeys

Always start the turkey breast-side down so the juices run into, rather than out of, the breast. The bacon prevents the breast from sticking to the roasting pan and adds a nice flavor to the juices. If, like most families, you enjoy lots of dressing (stuffing), make a double batch and bake it separately in a casserole dish while you are roasting the turkey.

Sesame-Crusted Chicken Breasts

Serve this with rice and lots of vegetables. Leftovers can be chopped, mixed with a spicy sauce, and used to fill Basic Crepes (Chapter 2) as a delicious snack.

SERVES 4

¼ cup pineapple juice

¼ cup orange juice

1 tablespoon lime juice

½ cup gluten-free soy sauce or soy-free Coconut Secret Coconut Aminos

1" gingerroot, peeled and minced or ½ teaspoon ground ginger

2 cloves garlic, minced

1 teaspoon chili oil, or to taste (optional)

2 large boneless, skinless chicken breasts, halved

1 egg, beaten

½ cup sesame seeds

1. In a nonreactive bowl or glass pan large enough to hold the chicken, whisk together the juices, soy sauce, ginger, garlic, and chili oil.

2. Rinse the chicken breasts and pat dry with paper towels. Add the chicken to the sauce and turn to coat. Cover and refrigerate for 4 hours.

3. Drain the chicken; dip in beaten egg and then in sesame seeds. Grill or sauté in oil for 6 minutes per side, depending on thickness of meat. Serve hot. Store any leftovers in an airtight container in the refrigerator for up to 3 days.

Chili and Other Hot Sauces

The Chinese, Indians, and other groups in Asia, Southeast Asia, and Asia Minor make their own versions of chili for cooking. Chili oil is extremely hot. Chili paste comes in green and red and is popular in Thailand. The Chinese also make a chili-and-garlic paste that is called Sichuan chili. Tabasco sauce, fresh chopped chilies (red and/or green), cayenne pepper, and red pepper flakes can be substituted. If your family does not like spice, it works well to leave out the chilies too!

Chicken Nuggets

These are a great snack when you have a group of children to feed. Your guests will not know they are being served special gluten-free chicken nuggets!

MAKES 16 NUGGETS

½ cup light-tasting olive oil

3 cups Rice Chex cereal (crushed)

¼ teaspoon hot paprika

½ teaspoon garlic salt

1 pound boneless, skinless chicken breasts, cut into strips

2 eggs, beaten

1. Heat oil in a medium skillet over high heat.

2. Place Rice Chex in gallon-sized plastic bag and crush; add paprika and garlic salt to bag and blend well.

3. Dip chicken strips in eggs, put in bag with Rice Chex and shake.

4. Fry chicken strips in oil until done, about 6–8 minutes, drain on paper towels and serve. Store any leftovers in an airtight container in the refrigerator for up to 3 days.

Fish Baked in Papillote

Fish is an excellent source of omega-3 fatty acids, which are great for overall health and important for healthy brains!

MAKES 4 FILLETS

4 teaspoons olive oil

8 sprigs fresh rosemary

4 fillets of Pacific halibut or other white fish

4 teaspoons capers

2 large tomatoes, chopped

1. Preheat oven to 350°F.

2. Lay out 4 pieces of parchment paper, each large enough to wrap around one fillet.

3. On each piece of parchment paper, spread out 1 teaspoon olive oil and 2 sprigs of rosemary.

4. Add 1 fillet on top of rosemary, top with capers and tomatoes.

5. Fold up paper and bake for about 10–15 minutes. Serve with baked potatoes and one of the homemade cole slaws from Chapter 4. Store any leftovers in an airtight container in the refrigerator for up to 3 days.

CHAPTER 7

VEGETARIAN ENTRÉES

Arroz Verde con Frijoles Negros

For a fun twist, serve this dish with warmed corn tortillas instead of forks.

MAKES 6 CUPS (6 SERVINGS)

5 cups gluten-free vegetable broth, divided

1 bay leaf

2 cups short-grain brown rice

1 bunch spinach

2 tablespoons lemon juice

2 cloves garlic

2 cups cooked black beans

Pepper, to taste

1. In a large saucepan, bring 4½ cups vegetable broth, bay leaf, and rice to a boil. Reduce heat, cover, and simmer 40 minutes.

2. While rice is cooking, thoroughly wash spinach and remove stems.

3. Combine spinach, lemon juice, and garlic in food processor. Process into a paste adding vegetable broth when necessary.

4. Remove bay leaf from rice, fluff with a fork, stir in drained and rinsed beans and spinach mixture.

5. Add pepper to taste. Serve with sliced avocados and chopped tomatoes on the side. Store any leftovers in an airtight container in the refrigerator for up to 3 days.

Barbecue White Beans and Quinoa

Quinoa and white beans combine for a protein-rich meal with a lot of flavor.

SERVES 4

1 cup quinoa

1 tablespoon olive oil

1 cup mushroom caps (button or cremini), diced

¼ small onion, diced

1 large red bell pepper, diced

1 (1-ounce) can white beans (cannellini beans or great northern beans), drained and rinsed

½ cup gluten-free barbecue sauce

1. Thoroughly rinse 1 cup quinoa. In a small saucepan, combine quinoa and 2 cups water. Bring to a boil. Reduce heat to simmer, cover, and cook 15 minutes.

2. In a large skillet, heat olive oil over high heat, then add mushrooms, onions, and red peppers. Sauté about 3–5 minutes until vegetables are softened.

3. Add white beans and cook 5 minutes more.

4. Add barbecue sauce and cook 5 more minutes.

5. Serve barbecue beans over quinoa. Store any leftovers in an airtight container in the refrigerator for up to 3 days.

Simple Barbecue Sauce

To make a tasty, basic barbecue sauce, combine ¼ cup gluten-free soy sauce or Coconut Secret Coconut Aminos, 2 tablespoons blackstrap molasses, 3 tablespoons honey or sugar, and ¼ cup ketchup.

Black Bean Cakes

You can substitute cornmeal for gluten-free bread crumbs in this recipe.

MAKES 6 CAKES

2 cups cooked black beans (or 1 [15-ounce] can)

3 tablespoons mild salsa

2 tablespoons cornmeal or gluten-free bread crumbs

1 tablespoon olive oil

1. Drain and rinse black beans. Place beans in a medium bowl and mash with a potato masher or fork.

2. Add the salsa and bread crumbs and mix well to combine. Form into 6 cakes.

3. In a medium skillet, heat oil over medium-high heat. Cook cakes till crispy on the outside and warm in the middle, about 5 minutes. These are best warm, the day they are made; however, you can store any leftovers in an airtight container in the refrigerator for up to 3 days.

Change Things Up!

Changing side dishes can completely change the tone of a meal. If you serve black bean cakes with a side of rice and avocado one day, try serving them for breakfast with fried or scrambled eggs the next time. Once you find something that your child likes, you can expand on that by serving the favored dish with different foods.

Broccoli Quinoa Casserole

This easy casserole is pure comfort food for the whole family. Children will love the creamy texture and mild taste. Imagine Food's Organic Sweet Corn Soup (which is gluten-free) has a nice consistency for this recipe. Or use the Creamy Corn Chowder in Chapter 5.

MAKES 6 CUPS
• • • • • • • • • • • • • • • •

1 cup creamy corn soup (try Imagine Foods's Organic Creamy Corn Soup or the "Creamy Corn Chowder" in Chapter 5) or canned cream corn, which is generally gluten-free

½ cup Cheddar cheese or nondairy alternative such as Daiya Cheddar cheese

1 large bunch of broccoli

3 cups cooked quinoa

1. In a small saucepan, heat soup over medium-high heat for 5–8 minutes until it's starting to heat through.

2. Add cheese and stir until melted. Set aside.

3. Cut broccoli into small florets and steam until tender.

4. In a large bowl combine quinoa, cheese sauce, and broccoli. Serve. If your children don't like to eat food combined into casseroles, simply serve all the ingredients separately and use the cheese sauce as a dipping sauce. Store any leftovers in an airtight container in the refrigerator for up to 3 days.

Is Quinoa a Grain?

Although quinoa looks like a grain and cooks like a grain, it is not a true cereal grain. It is actually the seeds of the Chenopodium, or goosefoot plant. Its relatives include beets, spinach, and Swiss chard.

Caribbean Baked Risotto

This dish is a complete meal incorporating fruit, vegetables, protein, and grains.

MAKES 4½ CUPS (6 SERVINGS)

1 cup Arborio rice

½ cup cooked black beans

1 clove garlic, minced

1 cup coconut milk

3 cups gluten-free vegetable broth

½ cup cooked pumpkin

1 cup pineapple pieces

1 cup chopped spinach

1. Preheat oven to 325°F.

2. Rinse rice. Drain and rinse beans.

3. Combine all ingredients in a covered casserole dish. Bake for 1 hour. Serve hot. Store any leftovers in an airtight container in the refrigerator for up to 3 days.

Risotto

Risotto is a traditional Italian creamy rice dish. It is typically made by stirring a small amount of hot liquid, usually broth or stock, into Arborio rice until the liquid is absorbed. This process continues until all of the liquid has been absorbed and the rice is fully cooked with a creamy, starch sauce. Baking Arborio rice brings about a similar result without standing in front of a stove for close to an hour. (A luxury not many parents can afford!)

Cheesy Polenta with Roasted Vegetables

Combining the creamy polenta with the tender roasted vegetables yields a comforting stew.

MAKES 5 CUPS (SERVES 4)

2 carrots

4 asparagus spears

6 mushrooms (button or cremini)

2 tablespoons olive oil

⅛ teaspoon salt

1 cup polenta or grits

3 cups water

½ cup Cheddar cheese or nondairy alternative such as Daiya Cheddar cheese

1. Preheat oven to 425°F.

2. Peel carrots and cut into ¼"-wide matchsticks. Break off tough ends of asparagus, and cut into 1"-long pieces. Cut mushrooms in half.

3. In a large bowl, toss vegetables in olive oil and salt.

4. Spread vegetables on baking sheet and cook until tender, approximately 10–15 minutes.

5. While vegetables are cooking, bring water to a boil in a medium saucepan. Slowly whisk in polenta and keep whisking until polenta thickens and pulls away from the sides of the pan.

6. Sprinkle cheese on polenta, and stir to melt.

7. In a large bowl, stir to combine polenta and vegetables. Store any leftovers in an airtight container in the refrigerator for up to 3 days.

Polenta, the Pasta of Northern Italy

Although Italy is known as the home of pasta and pizza, corn polenta has been a basic foodstuff since the late fifteenth century. Because corn, introduced to Italy from the New World, grows most easily in Northern Italy, polenta quickly became a culinary mainstay. It continues to be a very important component of Northern Italian cooking.

Corn Cakes with Black Bean Salsa

Serve each of these cornmeal pancakes with a dollop of the black bean salsa for a fun, breakfast-style dinner.

MAKES 6 SMALL PANCAKES

¼ cup cornmeal

½ cup brown rice flour

½ teaspoon xanthan gum

1 tablespoon flaxseed meal

2 tablespoons water

½ cup creamy corn soup (try Imagine Foods Organic Creamy Corn Soup or the Creamy Corn Chowder in Chapter 5) or canned cream corn

¼ cup milk or nondairy alternative such as unsweetened almond milk

2 teaspoons butter or coconut oil

1 cup mild salsa

¼ cup cooked black beans

1. In a medium bowl, combine cornmeal, flour, and xanthan gum.

2. In a separate bowl, mix flaxseed meal with water. Add room-temperature soup and milk and stir to combine.

3. Slowly mix dry ingredients into wet.

4. Melt 1 teaspoon butter in a skillet or griddle.

5. Drop batter to form approximately 2" pancakes onto hot pan.

6. When the edges firm up, flip pancakes and continue cooking on the other side.

7. While pancakes are cooking, combine salsa and drained and rinsed black beans in a small bowl.

8. Top each cooked pancake with salsa mixture. Serve with a fresh green salad and cantaloupe slices on the side. Store any leftovers in an airtight container in the refrigerator for up to 3 days.

Save Those Jars!

Jarred salsa tastes good and can be good for the environment, too. The size and shape is perfect for reusing as a food-storage container. Applesauce and pasta sauce jars also hold leftover soup, sauce, smoothies, and more. Reduce, reuse, and recycle has never been tastier!

Italian Eggplant

Gluten-free pasta tossed with olive oil makes a great complement to this entrée.

SERVES 8

1 large eggplant

1 tablespoon salt

1 cup cornmeal

½ teaspoon Italian seasoning

2 tablespoons olive oil

3 cups gluten-free pasta sauce

4 ounces shredded mozzarella cheese or nondairy alternative such as Daiya mozzarella cheese

1. Preheat oven to 350°F.

2. Thinly slice eggplant. (The slicing attachment on a food processor works well for this.) Sprinkle eggplant slices with salt, set aside for 20 minutes, then rinse.

3. In a medium bowl, combine cornmeal, Italian seasoning, and olive oil.

4. Toss eggplant in cornmeal mixture.

5. In a 9" × 13" lasagna pan, alternate layers of sauce and eggplant, beginning and ending with sauce.

6. Top with mozzarella cheese.

7. Bake for 50–60 minutes, until cheese is melted and eggplant is tender when pierced with a fork. Serve with the Cucumber Tomato Salad in Chapter 4 and gluten-free French bread. Store any leftovers in an airtight container in the refrigerator for up to 3 days.

To Peel or Not to Peel?

It is best to keep the skin on eggplant when cooking, as that is the part of the eggplant with the greatest amount of dietary fiber. To ensure that the skin will be tender after cooking, use young, smaller eggplants rather than older eggplants, which might have tougher skin.

Lentils and Brown Rice

This iron- and fiber-rich dish can be made into a wrap-style sandwich if wrapped in a gluten-free tortilla or the Basic Crepes in Chapter 2.

MAKES 3 CUPS (SERVES 6)

½ cup dried lentils

1 cup short-grain brown rice

2 cups gluten-free vegetable broth, such as Kitchen Basics brand

⅛ teaspoon cumin

2 tablespoons butter or coconut oil

1. Rinse and pick over lentils.

2. Combine lentils and rice in a medium saucepan.

3. Add gluten-free vegetable broth, cumin, and butter. Bring to a boil.

4. Cover, and reduce heat to a simmer. Cook 40 minutes until liquid has been absorbed and lentils are soft. Store any leftovers in an airtight container in the refrigerator for up to 3 days.

Lentils with Spinach and Quinoa

You do not want to mix old lentils with new lentils. The older lentils are, the longer they take to cook. Lentils will cook unevenly if you mix old and new lentils together.

MAKES 2 CUPS (SERVES 4)

½ cup uncooked quinoa

1 cup water

½ teaspoon minced garlic

1 teaspoon oil

1 cup dry lentils

Gluten-free vegetable broth to cover lentils

3 cups fresh spinach

1. Add quinoa and water in a microwaveable glass bowl. Cover and heat on high for 4 minutes. Remove from microwave and stir. Heat again for 2 minutes, stir, and let stand for 1 minute.

2. Pick out debris from lentils.

3. In a medium skillet over low-medium heat, sauté garlic in oil until translucent, about 3–4 minutes.

4. Add lentils to pan, cover with broth, and bring to a boil for 2–3 minutes. Reduce heat to medium and cook until the lentils are tender.

5. At end of lentils cooking, add spinach to broth.

6. Drain. Combine quinoa, lentils, and spinach. Serve with gluten-free toast and a fruit salad. Store any leftovers in an airtight container in the refrigerator for up to 3 days.

Lentil Cooking Tips

Wait! Do not add salt to the water in cooking your lentils as this might toughen the beans. Looking for another tip? Wait to add any acidic items to lentils until late in the cooking process as acidic foods make lentils take longer to cook.

Lentil-Stuffed Green Peppers

This entrée is packed with vitamin C and protein, and it's a crowd pleaser with family members of all ages.

MAKES 4 PEPPERS
. . . .
2 cups gluten-free pasta sauce

4 green bell peppers

1 recipe Lentils and Brown Rice (Chapter 7)

4 slices mozzarella cheese

1. Preheat oven to 350°F.

2. Spread ⅓ of the pasta sauce in the bottom of an 8" square pan.

3. Remove stems, seeds, and membranes from green peppers. Stuff peppers with lentil mixture.

4. Top peppers with cheese. Spread remainder of sauce over peppers.

5. Bake for 40 minutes.

Colorful Bell Peppers

Bell peppers are available in a rainbow of colors from green to red to purple. All bell peppers start out green. They change their color as they mature. This change in color also indicates a sweeter bell pepper. They make a sweet and colorful addition to salads, stir-fries, and sauces.

Mixed-Vegetable Stir-Fry

For a heartier dish, add 1 cup of the protein of your choice and serve over brown rice.

MAKES 5 CUPS

1 cup gluten-free vegetable broth

1 tablespoon gluten-free rice vinegar

1½ teaspoons gluten-free soy sauce (or try using Coconut Secret Coconut Aminos, a savory sauce that tastes very similar to soy sauce)

1 tablespoon cornstarch

2 tablespoons cold water

1–2 tablespoons olive oil

2 cloves garlic, minced

1¼" pieces of ginger, minced

2 carrots, chopped

½ onion, chopped

2 cups broccoli florets

1 cup bok choy, chopped

1 cup cabbage, chopped

1. In a small bowl, combine broth, vinegar, and soy sauce.

2. Dilute cornstarch in cold water and add to broth mixture.

3. In a wok or large frying pan, heat oil over high heat. Add garlic and ginger, and cook for 30 seconds.

4. Add carrots, onion, and broccoli. Cook for 2 minutes.

5. Add bok choy and cabbage. Cook for 1 minute.

6. Add sauce and cook for 2 minutes.

7. Cook until vegetables are tender, but not mushy. Instead of rice, try serving this dish with baked sweet potatoes or steamed spaghetti squash. Store any leftovers in an airtight container in the refrigerator for up to 3 days.

Brown Rice with Creamy Tomato Spinach Sauce

If using frozen spinach, thaw before using in this recipe.

MAKES 2½ CUPS (5 SERVINGS)

1 cup short-grain brown rice
½ cup gluten-free pasta sauce
¼ cup soaked cashews
2 tablespoons lemon juice
¼ cup chopped spinach

1. Bring 2 cups water to a boil. Add rice, reduce heat, and cover. Simmer covered for 40 minutes.

2. In a food processor, combine pasta sauce, soaked cashews, lemon juice, and spinach. Process until smooth.

3. Transfer sauce to a small saucepan. Heat through.

4. Stir rice into sauce. Serve with Green Salad with Home-made Egg-Free Caesar Dressing from Chapter 4. Store any leftovers in an airtight container in the refrigerator for up to 3 days.

Top Rice with Your Favorite Sauce

As a change from gluten-free pastas, think about topping rice with your favorite pasta sauces. Other ideas for pasta-sauce toppables include polenta, baked potatoes, or gluten-free toast.

Quinoa Primavera

This dish is easy to vary according to your family's tastes. You can make this dish with many different vegetables. Vary the produce options depending on the season for freshest flavor.

MAKES 8 CUPS (8 SERVINGS)

1½ cups quinoa

3 cups water

1 cup frozen corn, thawed

1 red pepper, finely chopped

1 green pepper, finely chopped

1 cucumber, finely chopped

Juice of 1 lemon

3 tablespoons flax oil or additional olive oil

3 tablespoons olive oil

3 tablespoons gluten-free rice wine vinegar

Salt, to taste

1. Rinse the quinoa under cold running water until the water runs clear.

2. In a medium saucepan, place quinoa and water. Turn on medium heat and cook for 10–15 minutes or until all the water is absorbed. Fluff with fork.

3. Combine quinoa with remaining ingredients. Mix thoroughly, chill, and serve with steamed broccoli and cauliflower. Store any leftovers in an airtight container in the refrigerator for up to 3 days.

What Is Rice Wine Vinegar?

Rice wine vinegar is a popular light vinegar that is widely used in Asian cuisine. It is a vinegar made from rice wine and has a mellow and slightly sweet flavor. It is a nice addition to marinades and vinaigrette dressings, or use it to drizzle over fish before cooking to give a light flavor.

Split Pea Curry

This is a very mild curry that is inspired by the flavorful curries that make up the heart of Indian cooking.

MAKES 5 CUPS

1½ teaspoons garam masala

1 clove garlic, minced

1 cup split peas

½ cup diced carrots

1 cup cauliflower florets

2 baking potatoes, diced

½ cup gluten-free tomato sauce

1 tablespoon olive oil

1. In a large sauté pan heat oil over medium heat and add garam masala and garlic. Heat for 3–4 minutes until the seasoning is aromatic and the garlic is soft. Add remaining ingredients to the pot and stir to combine.

2. Simmer for 45 minutes to 1 hour, or until peas are tender. Serve with a baby arugula salad and gluten-free French bread, unless you can find gluten-free pita bread, which is available in some large higher-end grocery stores in the frozen section. Store any leftovers in an airtight container in the refrigerator for up to 3 days.

Making the Most of a Slow Cooker

Even parents with the best of intentions for providing home-cooked meals for their families can become overwhelmed by all of the demands that life brings. A slow cooker can be a great tool to help reduce some of that pressure. Soups, casseroles, and curries can be assembled first thing in the morning or even the night before and then cook unattended for 6–8 hours.

Creamy Spinach Lasagna

Rice lasagna noodles will cook while the casserole is baking and don't need to be precooked.

MAKES A 9" SQUARE PAN (SERVES 9)
....

4 artichoke hearts

1 cup soaked cashews

1 tablespoon lemon juice

3–4 tablespoons water

2 cups chopped spinach

2 tablespoons plus 2 teaspoons olive oil, divided

1 tablespoon nutritional yeast

1 teaspoon garlic pepper

2 cups gluten-free pasta sauce

6 sheets gluten-free lasagna noodles

4 ounces mozzarella cheese or nondairy alternative such as Daiya mozzarella cheese

1. Preheat oven to 350°F. Finely chop artichoke hearts.

2. In a blender, mix together soaked cashews, lemon juice, and water.

3. In a large bowl, combine artichoke hearts, spinach, 1 tablespoon olive oil, nutritional yeast, garlic pepper, and cashew filling.

4. Spread a thin layer of pasta sauce in the bottom of a baking pan.

5. Alternate layers of sauce, uncooked noodles, and cashew filling. Finish with sauce and top with mozzarella.

6. Bake for 40 minutes until the top is golden brown and the filling is bubbly around the edges. Serve with a tossed salad and gluten-free French bread or biscuits. Store any leftovers in an airtight container in the refrigerator for up to 3 days.

Vegetable White Bean Pot Pie

Serve this warm, comforting dish with Strawberry Applesauce (Chapter 3) for dessert.

MAKES 6 CUPS

2 tablespoons olive oil

2–3 potatoes, peeled and chopped into bite-size pieces

2 carrots, chopped

1 small onion, chopped

1 cup broccoli florets

4 large mushrooms, chopped

1½ cups gluten-free vegetable broth

1 tablespoon nutritional yeast

1 tablespoon garlic pepper

1 tablespoon poultry seasoning

1 teaspoon dried dill

1 tablespoon cornstarch

2 tablespoons cold water

1 (1-ounce) can white beans, drained and rinsed

1 frozen gluten-free pie crust or use Pie Pastry recipe (Chapter 2)

2 tablespoons melted butter or additional olive oil

1. Preheat oven to 350°F.

2. Heat olive oil in a skillet over medium-high heat and add potatoes, carrots, onion, and broccoli. Sauté for 3–5 minutes, until slightly soft. Add mushrooms, sauté 1 more minute.

3. In a medium bowl, mix together broth, nutritional yeast, and spices.

4. Dilute cornstarch with cold water. Add to broth mixture.

5. Toss vegetables and white beans with sauce.

6. Pour mixture into 2-quart casserole.

7. Add pie crust to top of casserole; pinch edges around top of dish. Prick pie crust with a fork. Brush top of pie crust with melted butter or olive oil.

8. Bake for 45–55 minutes, or until crust is golden and sauce is bubbling through holes in the crust. Store any leftovers in an airtight container in the refrigerator for up to 3 days.

Nutritional Yeast

Nutritional yeast is used as a flavoring agent and as a nutritional supplement, as it provides protein and B vitamins. Some nutritional yeast is enriched with Vitamin B12. Do not confuse inactive nutritional yeast with active yeast, such as baker's yeast. Active yeasts should not be consumed raw.

Shells with Marinara Sauce

This is a wonderful homemade marinara sauce; easy and versatile! Use this sauce in the Italian Eggplant recipe (this chapter).

MAKES 3 CUPS OF SAUCE (SERVES 6)

1 tablespoon olive oil

1 clove garlic, minced

2½ cups diced tomatoes (or 1 [28-ounce] can diced tomatoes, drained)

3 ounces tomato paste

1 teaspoon sugar

1 tablespoon fresh basil (or 1 teaspoon dried basil)

1 teaspoon dried oregano

3 cups cooked gluten-free pasta

1. In a medium saucepan, heat olive oil over medium heat. Add garlic; sauté for 2 minutes, until fragrant.

2. Add remaining ingredients; stir thoroughly.

3. Simmer uncovered for approximately 1 hour or until desired texture.

4. Serve sauce over cooked pasta. Serve with steamed green beans and fresh corn on the cob.

Macaroni and Cheese

Surprisingly, giving up gluten does not have to mean giving up creamy macaroni and cheese.

SERVES 8

8 cups (2 [32-ounce] boxes) gluten-free vegetable broth

1 pound gluten-free pasta (elbow macaroni, rotini, penne, or other short shape)

1 (10-ounce) package Cheddar cheese, shredded

1. In a large saucepan, bring broth to a boil. Add pasta and cook according to package directions.

2. While pasta cooks, remove ⅓ cup of broth and transfer it to another large saucepan.

3. Add chopped cheese and cook over medium heat. Stir regularly until cheese melts.

4. When pasta is done cooking, remove pasta with a slotted spoon and transfer to cheese.

5. Toss pasta with melted cheese until well coated. Serve with buttered peas and carrots and fresh homemade applesauce. Store any leftovers in an airtight container in the refrigerator for up to 3 days.

CHAPTER 8

SANDWICHES AND SNACKS

Barbecue Chicken Pizza

Prebaking the pizza crust helps this pizza not become soggy. You can either make a homemade Best Pizza Crust (see Chapter 2) or buy a gluten-free crust at the store. Either way, bake it before adding toppings.

MAKES 4 SERVINGS

3 tablespoons gluten-free barbecue sauce

½ cup marinara sauce

1 prebaked gluten-free pizza crust such as Udi's (or Best Pizza Crust; see Chapter 2)

8 ounces shredded chicken

⅓ cup red onion, sliced thin

1½ cups mozzarella cheese or nondairy alternative such as Daiya mozzarella cheese (optional)

2 tablespoons chopped cilantro (optional)

1. Preheat oven to 425°F.

2. In small bowl, combine barbecue sauce and marinara sauce. Spread on prebaked pizza crust.

3. Top pizza with chicken and red onions and cheese, if using. Bake about 15 minutes.

4. Remove from oven, sprinkle with cilantro, if using. Cool for 10 minutes and serve. Store any leftovers in an airtight container in the refrigerator for up to 3 days.

Black Bean Roll-Ups

Using a 4-ounce jar of baby food carrots in this recipe makes assembling these tasty sandwiches a breeze.

MAKES 6 TORTILLAS

1 teaspoon olive oil

¼ cup onions, minced

1 teaspoon garlic, minced

1 (15-ounce) can black beans, drained and rinsed

4 ounces (1 small jar) carrot purée

1 teaspoon cumin

6 corn tortillas

½ avocado, mashed

1. Heat olive oil in skillet over medium-high heat. Add onion and garlic to skillet and sauté until clear.
2. Drain and rinse can of black beans.
3. Add black beans, carrot purée, and cumin to the skillet.
4. Mash with potato masher until desired consistency is reached.
5. Heat until heated through and remove from heat.
6. Heat tortillas in a dry skillet over medium heat.
7. Top each tortilla with a thin layer of bean spread and then mashed avocado.
8. Roll tortillas from end to end to make a spiral. Use a little water on the end to make them stick if needed.
9. Cut at diagonals into about 3 pieces and serve. These wraps do not store in the refrigerator well.

Birthday or Sleepover Party Food

Spirals or roll-ups are typically a hit with children. You can make several different types of roll-ups and cut them into bite-size pieces. Arrange them on a plate and let your child and friends dig in! Children may be more willing to try new foods when they see other children try them . . . peer pressure in reverse!

Caribbean Dream Boats

Although celery is 95 percent water, this powerhouse vegetable also provides fiber, folate, and potassium. It is a great gluten-free vehicle for serving spreads and dips.

MAKES 12 BOATS (12 SERVINGS)

4 washed celery stalks

1 (8-ounce) package cream cheese or nondairy alternative such as Daiya cream cheese

1 (8-ounce) can crushed organic pineapple, drained

¼ cup shredded coconut

Tropical drink umbrellas

1. Trim celery stalks; wash and dry thoroughly.
2. Cut into 4" pieces.
3. Combine cream cheese and pineapple in a bowl with a spatula.
4. Spoon 2 tablespoons into celery and level with a knife.
5. Sprinkle lightly with coconut.
6. Top each with a tropical drink umbrella.
7. Cover, chill, and serve. These are best the day they are made.

Mix It Up!

Creativity goes a long way with children. Have fun making different arrangements with their food to tempt them to try new things. Make faces on pizzas or tortillas with vegetables, or make a "scene" with their whole plate! Let your children create art with their food, and then watch them eat it!

Creamy Spinach Mini Pizzas

Creamed spinach takes the place of traditional pizza sauce in this alternative Italian-style pie.

MAKES 2 PIZZAS

Gluten-free bagel, such as Udi's

¼ cup Creamed Spinach (Chapter 9)

2 slices tomato

1 tablespoon Parmesan cheese or nondairy alternative such as blanched almond flour(optional)

1. Cut bagel in half, and toast.

2. Spread spinach on each bagel half.

3. Top with tomato.

4. Sprinkle on Parmesan, if using.

5. Broil for 2 minutes; watch to prevent burning. Allow to cool briefly and then serve.

Pizza Crust Ideas

Consider these ideas to form the base of a pizza: Gluten-free bagel, gluten-free prepared pizza crust, corn tortilla, gluten-free waffle, or gluten-free toast. With a little imagination, a pizza party is always possible.

Eggy Boats

One simple way to make the butternut squash purée is to use jarred baby food as a substitute. Baby food purées can be a healthy addition to your kitchen long after your children have outgrown baby food!

**MAKES 25 BOATS
(SERVING 2 BOATS)**
••••••••••••••••••••
25 snow pea pods

6 hard-boiled eggs

¼ cup mayonnaise

2 tablespoons butternut squash purée

Salt and pepper to taste

½ cup olive slices

1. Wash pea pods and dry thoroughly.

2. Slice the top of the pea pod (the straight side) open so you make "pea pod boats."

3. Mash hard-boiled eggs and mix together with the mayonnaise and butternut squash with a fork.

4. Add salt and pepper to taste.

5. Spoon 1 tablespoon into each pea pod and top with olive slices as "lifesavers."

6. Cover, chill, and serve.

Pizza Toast

The sky's the limit as to what other toppings you can use to customize these little pizzas. Try bell peppers, mushrooms, or even pineapple for a yummy treat.

MAKES 2 PIZZAS

¼ cup gluten-free pizza sauce

2 pieces of gluten-free bread such as Udi's, toasted (or try the Basic Sandwich Bread in Chapter 2)

2 slices mozzarella cheese or nondairy alternative such as Daiya mozzarella cheese

1. Preheat oven or toaster oven to 400°F.

2. Spread half of the sauce on each piece of bread.

3. Top with cheese.

4. Cook until cheese is melted and toast is golden brown, 5–7 minutes. Allow to cool briefly and serve.

Easy, Kid-Friendly Pizza Sauce

Combine 1 can tomato paste, ½ teaspoon garlic powder, ½ teaspoon oregano, ½ teaspoon basil, and ¾ teaspoon agave nectar or sugar, for a tasty, easy pizza sauce. Store extra sauce in an airtight container in the refrigerator.

Hummus and Mango Sandwich

This creamy, sweet, and savory sandwich provides protein, fiber, iron, and vitamins A and C.

MAKES 1 SANDWICH

2 pieces gluten-free bread

2 tablespoons Hummus (Chapter 11)

¼ cup mango slices

1. Lightly toast bread. Make sure to use a dedicated gluten-free toaster.

2. Spread Hummus over the surface of both pieces of bread.

3. Top one piece with mango slices.

4. Top with other piece of toast.

5. Cut sandwich in half and serve.

How to Choose a Mango

When selecting a mango, two senses come into play to determine which fruit is best. First, smell the mango at the stem end. It should have a nice fruity aroma. Second, touch the mango. It should feel firm, yet yield to gentle pressure in much the same way as a peach.

Pinto Bean Burgers

Having a hard time finding gluten-free bread crumbs? Make your own! To make bread crumbs, toast gluten-free bread, then let cool. Once cool, process until crumbly. You can also use crushed gluten-free corn tortilla chips.

MAKES 4–6 BURGERS
....

1 (15-ounce) can pinto beans (or 2 cups cooked)

½ medium green pepper

½ medium onion

2 cloves garlic

1 tablespoon olive oil

1 tablespoon flaxseed meal

3 tablespoons water

½ cup gluten-free bread crumbs

2 teaspoons olive oil

1. Drain and rinse beans. Mince green pepper, onion, and garlic.

2. In a medium skillet, heat 1 tablespoon olive oil over medium-high flame. Add vegetables and sauté until soft, approximately 3–5 minutes. Add beans and heat through.

3. Scrape bean mixture in a large bowl.

4. Mash bean mixture with a potato masher or fork.

5. Remove skillet from heat and set aside.

6. In a small bowl, combine flaxseed meal and water.

7. Combine bean mixture, flaxseed meal mixture, and bread crumbs.

8. Form mixture into patties.

9. Add olive oil to skillet. Heat over medium flame.

10. Cook patties, turning occasionally, until browned on both sides. Serve on gluten-free buns with your favorite burger toppings. Store any leftovers in an airtight container in the refrigerator for up to 3 days.

Pinto Bean Roll-Up

This is a quick and healthy lunch! Serve these for friends and they will not even know you are making a gluten-free lunch! These are excellent dipped in the Creamy Salsa Dip (Chapter 11).

MAKES 1 TORTILLA

1 corn tortilla

2 tablespoons pinto bean purée

2 tablespoons shredded carrots

2 tablespoons shredded cabbage

1. Warm tortilla in a dry pan over medium heat.

2. Spread pinto bean purée over the surface of the tortilla.

3. Sprinkle on carrots and cabbage.

4. Tightly roll tortilla into a tube.

5. Cut tortilla tube into three 2" pieces and serve.

Quesadilla with Tomato

For a change, substitute refried pinto beans for Cheddar cheese.

MAKES 1 QUESADILLA

½ ripe avocado

2 corn tortillas

1 ripe tomato

¼ cup shredded Cheddar cheese or nondairy alternative such as Daiya cheddar cheese

¼ cup salsa

1. Cut avocado and scrape out the insides. Mash avocado with a fork.

2. Add avocado mash on the tortilla.

3. Dice tomato and layer on top of avocado.

4. Sprinkle cheese on top of this layer and top with second tortilla.

5. Heat dry skillet over medium-high flame. Place quesadilla in skillet. Heat until cheese begins to melt. Flip and cook to golden brown. Remove from heat and cut into 4 triangles.

6. Top with salsa and serve.

Secret Beef Burgers

Serve these on your favorite gluten-free bun! No plum purée? A handful of fresh blueberries can also have the same effects on the ground beef and boost the nutrition content of the hamburgers.

MAKES 4 BURGERS

1 pound lean ground beef

3 tablespoons organic baby food plum purée

1 tablespoon flaxseed meal

⅓ cup onions, minced

Sea salt, to taste

Freshly ground black pepper, to taste

1. Combine ground beef, baby food, flax meal, and onions; mix lightly but thoroughly.

2. Shape loosely into four ½"-thick patties. Season with sea salt and pepper to taste.

3. Cook patties immediately after mixing meat mixture for best results. Heat large skillet about 2 minutes over medium heat until hot. Cook patties 10–12 minutes to desired doneness, turning once.

4. Serve burgers on whole-wheat buns with romaine or spinach lettuce, fresh tomatoes, and condiments if desired.

Prunes in a Burger?

Adding prunes to your burgers may sound surprising! Prunes keep the meat very moist and add a very subtle sweet taste to the burger. Your children will not know that you are providing them a great source of antioxidants.

Cashew Avocado Spread

This creamy spread is rich in protein and potassium and pairs nicely with a piece of gluten-free toast, or dip your homemade corn tortilla chips in this tasty dip.

MAKES ½ CUP
. . . .

⅓ cup soaked cashews

1 tablespoon lemon juice

½ ripe avocado

¼ teaspoon gluten-free soy sauce or soy-free Coconut Secret Coconut Aminos

1. Add soaked cashews with lemon juice in a blender. Purée on high speed. Add avocado and soy sauce and blend until smooth.

2. Use as a dip or a sandwich spread. Store any leftovers in an airtight container in the refrigerator for up to 3 days.

Crunchy Black Bean Bites

Who needs highly processed chicken nuggets, when these tasty, high-protein, gluten-free treats are so easy to make?

MAKES 24 BITES
(SERVING SIZE = 6 BITES)

1 (1-ounce) can black beans, drained and rinsed

1 egg or 1 tablespoon of ground flaxseeds mixed with 3 tablespoons warm water, set aside to gel

¼ cup gluten-free cornmeal (ground fine)

1 teaspoon garlic pepper

½ teaspoon sea salt

3–4 tablespoons olive oil, divided

1. Preheat oven to 425°F.

2. In a large bowl, mash black beans and mix with egg or flaxseed gel. Scoop out mixture into 24 round balls.

3. Combine cornmeal, garlic pepper, and sea salt in a shallow bowl.

4. Dredge each black bean ball through the cornmeal mixture, until they are thoroughly coated.

5. Spread 1 tablespoon olive oil on a cookie sheet or line with a sheet of parchment paper. Brush remaining olive oil gently over each ball.

6. Bake black bean bites for 10–15 minutes or until golden brown and crunchy. These bites are best the day they are made.

Turkey Avocado Roll-Up

Pack these in a lunchbox. Many children love to pull apart wraps and sandwiches and eat all the components separately. Playing with food is a great way for children to explore and accept new tastes and textures!

MAKES 6 TORTILLAS

6 corn tortillas

1 ripe avocado, mashed

12 ounces oven-roasted turkey, sliced

2 cups red cabbage, shredded

1 cucumber, sliced

2 carrots, shredded

Rice wine vinegar

1. Warm each tortilla in a dry skillet over medium heat.

2. Top each one with 2 tablespoons of avocado and spread evenly over tortilla.

3. Top with 3 ounces of turkey, ⅓ cup shredded cabbage, slices of cucumber, and shredded carrots.

4. Sprinkle rice wine vinegar to taste.

5. Roll up tortilla and slice across each tortilla to make 2 smaller wraps and serve.

Veggie Roll-Up

This wrap-style sandwich combines textures in a really appealing way.

MAKES 2 TORTILLAS

2 corn tortillas

4 tablespoons Cashew Avocado Spread (Chapter 8)

2 tablespoons chopped tomato

2 tablespoons minced red pepper

2 tablespoons chopped cucumber

1. Spread Cashew Avocado Spread across surface of the tortilla.

2. Sprinkle on vegetables.

3. Tightly roll tortilla into a tube.

4. Cut the tube in half and serve.

Curried Chicken

This Middle Eastern–inspired chicken can be served wrapped in the Basic Crepes from Chapter 2 or in large lettuce leaves. Serve with grapes and apple slices.

SERVES 8

1 recipe Basic Crepes (see Chapter 2) or large lettuce leaves

½ pound chicken breast, poached for 10 minutes, or leftover cooked chicken, minced

2 teaspoons curry powder, or to taste

½ cup yogurt or nondairy alternative such as So Delicious Coconut Milk Yogurt

¼ cup mango chutney

1. Stack the crepes with waxed paper between them. Mix together the chicken, curry powder, yogurt, and chutney. Place a spoonful of the chicken curry mixture on a quarter section of each crepe.

2. Fold in quarters. Place on a platter and serve.

Zucchini Yacht

This recipe makes a great dish for a group. Serve this with Eggy Boats (see this chapter) and Caribbean Dream Boats (see this chapter) and have a boat parade for your children!

MAKES 2 YACHTS

1 zucchini

1 summer yellow squash, chopped

¼ red onion, chopped

1 ripe mango

½ cup finely chopped cilantro

2 tablespoons gluten-free red wine vinegar

1 tablespoon olive oil

1. Slice zucchini lengthwise forming 2 long boats.

2. Scrape out shallow middle of the zucchini to form the hull of the boat.

3. Combine yellow squash, onion, mango, and cilantro and mix with red wine vinegar, and olive oil until coated thoroughly.

4. Fill the zucchini boats with this filling.

5. Serve on a slice of romaine lettuce for the "water."

Zucchini Vessels

Hollowed-out zucchinis make great vessels to hold different foods. Fill the zucchini with egg salad, chicken salad, or a fruit salad. Nutritionally, your children will get small amounts of folate, potassium, vitamin A, and manganese when eating zucchini.

Spicy Meatballs

Meatballs always have bread as a filler and sometimes as an outside coating. Here, you'll use ground potato chips. The eggs will hold the balls together, and the ground chips give them a crispy, crunchy exterior.

MAKES 10–12 MEATBALLS

1 pound lean ground beef

1 egg

2 cloves garlic, minced

1 teaspoon dried oregano

½ teaspoon cinnamon

½ teaspoon fennel seeds

½ cup finely grated Parmesan cheese or a nondairy alternative such as blanched almond meal

Salt and pepper to taste

2 cups crushed low-salt potato chips, divided

Light-tasting olive oil, for frying

1. In a large bowl, mix all ingredients except 1 cup of the chip crumbs and the cooking oil.

2. Place a large sheet of waxed paper on the counter. Sprinkle remaining cup of chip crumbs on it.

3. Form meatballs, roll in crumbs, and fry them in oil until well browned. Drain on paper towels and then either refrigerate, freeze, or serve with the marinara sauce of your choice. Store any leftovers in an airtight container in the refrigerator for up to 3 days.

Spicy Meatballs

You can add flavor to your meatballs by grinding up some sweet or hot Italian sausage and mixing it with the beef. A truly great Italian sausage has aromatics like garlic, and herbs and spices such as anise seeds.

Fried Polenta Squares with Salsa

Make the polenta a day in advance, then refrigerate it until just before the party.

MAKES 12 SQUARES

6½ cups water

2 tablespoons salt

2 cups yellow gluten-free cornmeal

2–4 ounces butter

2 tablespoons dried herbs or 1 tablespoon each fresh: basil, rosemary, and parsley

½ cup Parmesan cheese or nondairy alternative such as blanched almond flour

Freshly ground black pepper to taste

4–6 tablespoons olive oil, for frying

1 (8-ounce) jar of your favorite salsa or homemade Guacamole (Chapter 11) for dipping

1. Bring the water to a boil.

2. Add salt, and using your hand, drop the cornmeal into the boiling water, letting it slip slowly between your fingers to make a very slim stream. You should be able to see each grain. Do not dump the cornmeal into the water or you will get a mass of glue.

3. Stir constantly while adding the cornmeal. Reduce heat to a simmer and keep stirring for about 20 minutes as it thickens.

4. Stir in the butter, herbs, Parmesan cheese, and pepper. Spread in a 9" × 13" glass pan that has been prepared with nonstick spray.

5. Chill for 3 hours or overnight. Cut into squares and fry until golden brown over medium heat in oil. If you are having an outdoor party, you can grill the squares over low flame for a smoky flavor. Serve with salsa or Guacamole (see Chapter 11). Store any leftovers in an airtight container in the refrigerator for up to 3 days.

Homemade Potato Chips

These are just too good and will be grabbed fast, so plan to make extra.

**MAKES ABOUT 50 CHIPS
(SERVING = 10 CHIPS)**

4 large Yukon Gold potatoes

1 cup light-tasting olive oil

Salt to taste

1. Peel and slice the potatoes. The best way to slice these chips is with a mandoline or the slicing blade on your food processor.

2. Place 2" of oil in the fryer. Heat the oil to 340°F and watch the temperature throughout the cooking time.

3. Carefully add potato slices, a few at a time, to hot oil. Remove when golden and drain on brown paper bags or paper towels. Sprinkle with salt. Serve hot or warm. (For a variation, mix 2 teaspoons chili powder with 2 teaspoons salt and sprinkle on the chips as they cool.) These chips do not store well, so only make as many as you can enjoy in one sitting.

CHAPTER 9

VEGETABLE SIDES

Vegetable Baked Risotto

This delicious dish delivers protein, iron, fiber, and a variety of vitamins.

MAKES 4½ CUPS (SERVES 6)

3 cups gluten-free vegetable broth

½ cup green beans

1 cup Arborio rice

1 cup broccoli florets

1 small zucchini

1 clove garlic

1 cup cooked great northern beans

1 teaspoon dried basil

1 teaspoon dried oregano

1. Preheat oven to 325°F.

2. Bring broth to a boil.

3. Drain and rinse green beans and rinse rice.

4. Trim ends from green beans; cut into 1" pieces.

5. Divide broccoli into small florets, and coarsely chop zucchini.

6. Mince garlic.

7. Drain and rinse great northern beans.

8. Combine all ingredients in a covered casserole. Bake 1 hour or until most of the liquid has been absorbed and the rice is cooked through, but still has a toothsome bite. Store any leftovers in an airtight container in the refrigerator for up to 3 days.

Herbed Broccoli

Save the stalks from the broccoli and use them to make vegetable broth.

MAKES 2½ CUPS

Large head of broccoli
¼ cup gluten-free vegetable broth
¼ teaspoon basil, dried
¼ teaspoon oregano, dried
⅛ teaspoon thyme, dried
⅛ teaspoon savory, dried

1. Cut bite-size florets from the head of broccoli.
2. Toss florets with broth and herbs.
3. Steam in microwave 3 minutes or in a steamer basket until desired tenderness. Store any leftovers in an airtight container in the refrigerator for up to 3 days.

Apple-Roasted Carrots

If your child is a reluctant utensil user, carrot slices make a good finger food. You can also use these for dips!

MAKES ¾ CUP

4 large carrots
¼ cup apple juice concentrate

1. Peel and thinly slice carrots.
2. Preheat oven to 450°F.
3. Toss carrots with apple juice concentrate.
4. Bake 10–12 minutes, or until carrots are tender. Store any leftovers in an airtight container in the refrigerator for up to 3 days.

Hawaiian Sweet Potatoes

Roasting the sweet potatoes with the pineapple gives this dish a festive air without any added sugar.

MAKES 2 CUPS (SERVES 2)

1 large sweet potato
1 cup chopped pineapple

1. Preheat oven to 375°F.
2. Wash sweet potato and cut into wedges lengthwise.
3. Arrange sweet potato wedges in a small baking dish.
4. Cover sweet potatoes with pineapple pieces and juice.
5. Bake 45–55 minutes, or until sweet potatoes are very tender. Store any leftovers in an airtight container in the refrigerator for up to 3 days.

The World-Traveling Pineapple
Although pineapples are native to Paraguay and Brazil, they made their way around the world on sailing vessels. Sailors ate them to prevent scurvy. The same vitamin C that helped sailors helps keep today's little ones healthy.

Cauliflower and Potato Mash

Here is a twist on mashed potatoes! Add other items to these "mashed potatoes" based on your child's taste. Try adding peas to this mash for a little more texture.

MAKES 5 CUPS

2 large potatoes, chopped

1 head of cauliflower, cut into florets

1 cup milk or nondairy alternative such as unsweetened almond milk or rice milk

¼ cup butter or coconut oil

½ teaspoon sea salt

½ teaspoon freshly ground black pepper

1. Place potatoes in a medium pot and cover with water. Boil the potatoes for 10 minutes until soft, drain, and return to pot.

2. Steam the cauliflower until tender, drain, and add to pot with potatoes.

3. Add milk and butter, salt, and pepper to potatoes and cauliflower.

4. Mash with a potato masher or use a beater to get a thinner purée. Serve while warm. Mashed potatoes get cold quickly, so make sure this is the last thing you prepare for your meal. Store any leftovers in an airtight container in the refrigerator for up to 3 days.

Are There Different Colors of Cauliflower?

Yes, there are! There is a purple cauliflower that contains the antioxidant anthocyanin, which is also in red wine and cabbage. There is green cauliflower, which is called broccoflower. And there is orange cauliflower, which contains 25 times more vitamin A than white cauliflower . . . it competes well with carrots!

Creamed Spinach

Serve this creamed spinach on a baked potato for a more filling dish.

SERVES 3

1 bunch spinach

½ gluten-free dinner roll

2 tablespoons olive oil

1 clove garlic

2 tablespoons brown rice flour

½ teaspoon salt

¼ teaspoon pepper

2–4 tablespoons milk or nondairy alternative such as unsweetened almond milk or rice milk

1. Thoroughly wash spinach and remove stems.
2. Roughly chop spinach.
3. Wilt spinach in a dry skillet over medium heat.
4. Combine wilted spinach with roll in a food processor.
5. Process until finely chopped.
6. Heat olive oil over medium flame.
7. Sauté minced garlic until fragrant.
8. Add flour, then salt and pepper.
9. Add 2 tablespoons milk.
10. Add spinach mixture.
11. If necessary, add more milk until desired consistency.
12. Heat through and serve immediately. Store any leftovers in an airtight container in the refrigerator for up to 3 days.

Toppings for a Baked Potato

Creamed spinach, chili, or even pasta sauce all help potatoes take center stage on the dinner plate. Olive oil is also a tasty condiment for a baked potato, especially when you're dining out.

Frosted Cauliflower

For a more striking presentation, this can be made with the whole head intact and then divided into florets when serving.

MAKES 3 CUPS (4 SERVINGS)

1 head cauliflower

¼ cup plain yogurt or nondairy alternative such as So Delicious Coconut Milk Yogurt

2 tablespoons yellow mustard

1 teaspoon honey

½ cup shredded Cheddar cheese or nondairy alternative such as Daiya Cheddar cheese

1. Preheat oven to 350°F.

2. Bring a large pot of water to a boil.

3. Cut cauliflower into florets.

4. Drop florets into boiling water; cook for 1–2 minutes. Drain and rinse under cold water.

5. In a small bowl, mix together yogurt, mustard, and honey.

6. Toss cauliflower in sauce.

7. Transfer to 1½-quart casserole dish and cover with cheese.

8. Bake, uncovered, for 20–25 minutes, or until cheese is melted. Store any leftovers in an airtight container in the refrigerator for up to 3 days.

Orange Beets

How to boil your own beets: First, cut off the tops and 1" of stem. Wash beets but do not peel. Place in pot with boiling water and cook for ½–2 hours. The skins slip off easily when done.

MAKES 4 CUPS

1 (8-ounce) package peeled and steamed ready-to-eat baby beets

1 can (6-ounce) mandarin oranges

1 fresh apple, cut into slices

¼ cup light-tasting olive oil

3 tablespoons orange juice

1 tablespoon lemon juice

1 teaspoon orange zest

1. Slice beets into tiny small slices.

2. In large mixing bowl, combine beets with mandarin oranges and apples.

3. In a small bowl, combine oil, orange juice, and lemon juice.

4. Toss dressing over fruit and chill. Serve. Store any leftovers in an airtight container in the refrigerator for up to 3 days. This makes a great side dish to take for school lunches.

Beets Not Your Child's Favorite Food?

It can take a while for your child to develop a taste for beets. Beets have one of the highest natural sugar contents of any vegetable, so they are great for roasting. Try roasting beets to bring out a sweeter flavor that might tempt your child. You can also try canned beets and see if they are accepted.

Grilled Summer Vegetables

Grill vegetables on the top rack of the grill. Don't choose vegetables with a high water content, like cucumbers. They will not grill well. Stick to heartier vegetables and fruits to grill.

MAKES 4 CUPS

1 head broccoli, trimmed into florets

1 yellow summer squash, sliced

3 fresh ripe tomatoes, cut into wedges

1 red onion, sliced

½ cup gluten-free Italian dressing

¼ teaspoon sea salt

1. Combine all ingredients.

2. Wrap in aluminum foil.

3. Place on top rack of hot grill for 5–7 minutes or until vegetables are tender.

4. Remove from heat and transfer to serving bowl.

Check the Label on Your Salad Dressing

Many Italian dressings are basically oil, vinegar, spices, and sweeteners. Always check the ingredients, though, to ensure that there isn't any cheese or gluten (barley malt, in particular) in the brand you're using. Remember to check the label every time you buy even a trusted brand, because ingredients can change with no notice.

Honeyed Carrots

This is another great way to provide carrots with a little extra sweetness.

**MAKES 1 POUND OF CARROTS
(8 SERVINGS)**
• • • • • • • • • • • • • • • •

1 pound carrot coins, steamed

1 tablespoon butter

4 tablespoons honey

1 tablespoon lemon or lime juice

1. Steam carrot coins in the microwave until tender.

2. In medium saucepan over medium heat, melt butter.

3. In small bowl, combine honey, and lemon or lime juice.

4. Add carrots and honey mixture to saucepan with butter. Heat through and mix until coated with honey mixture.

5. Remove with slotted spoon and serve. Sprinkle with salt to taste. Store any leftovers in an airtight container in the refrigerator for up to 3 days.

Maple Acorn Squash

Cooking acorn squash in a water bath results in an extremely tender side dish.

MAKES 2 HALVES

1 acorn squash

2 tablespoons pure maple syrup

2 tablespoons brown sugar

2 tablespoons butter or coconut oil

1. Preheat oven to 375°F.

2. Cut squash in half; scoop out seeds and discard.

3. Place squash cut-side down in a square baking pan.

4. Fill with water until it is 1"–2" deep.

5. Bake 45 minutes or until flesh is very tender.

6. Pour off water, turn squash cut-side up and pour 1 table-spoon maple syrup, 1 tablespoon of brown sugar, and 1 tablespoon of butter into each half.

7. Turn oven to broiler setting. Broil 2 minutes. Serve. Store any leftovers in an airtight container in the refrigerator for up to 3 days.

Mashed Potatoes and Parsnips

Yukon Gold potatoes have a rich flavor, creamy texture, and beautiful color.

MAKES 3 CUPS (6 SERVINGS)

4 Yukon Gold potatoes

2 parsnips

3 tablespoons olive oil

½ teaspoon sea salt, optional

1. Peel potatoes and parsnips.

2. Roughly chop vegetables and place in a medium saucepan.

3. Cover with water.

4. Bring to a boil, then reduce heat to a simmer.

5. Cook until vegetables are tender, approximately 10–15 minutes, depending on size of chopped pieces.

6. Drain, reserving cooking liquid.

7. Return vegetables to pot, mash with a potato masher or fork; stir in olive oil and salt if using.

8. Add reserved cooking water, one tablespoon at a time, until mash is the desired consistency. Serve while warm. Store any leftovers in an airtight container in the refrigerator for up to 3 days.

Parsnips, a Late-Fall Treat

Parsnips look very similar to white carrots. Because they are at their sweetest after having been exposed to cold temperatures, they are best in the late fall or early winter. Cook them in the same way as carrots for great-tasting results.

Mashed "Sweet" Potatoes

These mashed sweet potatoes are perfect not only as a holiday side dish, but could easily pass for a healthy dessert. Serve with crumbled gluten-free graham crackers on top for an afternoon snack.

MAKES 4 CUPS (8 SERVINGS)

4 sweet potatoes, peeled

¼ cup butter or coconut oil

¼ cup honey

¼ cup brown sugar

½ cup milk or nondairy alternative such as almond milk or coconut milk

1. Peel potatoes and cube them.

2. Bring pot of water to a boil. Place potatoes in boiling water and boil for about 20 minutes.

3. Drain potatoes and place in mixing bowl.

4. Add butter, honey, and brown sugar, mix well.

5. Add milk and stir to reach desired texture. Store any leftovers in an airtight container in the refrigerator for up to 3 days.

Roasted Potato Rounds

Baking potatoes or Yukon Gold potatoes can be substituted for red potatoes.

**MAKES 24 ROUNDS
(4 SERVINGS)**

3 large red potatoes

2 tablespoons olive oil

Sprinkling of sea salt

1. Preheat oven to 475°F.

2. Wash and thinly slice potatoes.

3. Spread 1 tablespoon olive oil on baking sheet.

4. Spread potato slices on top of oil.

5. Top with remaining oil and salt.

6. Bake 15–25 minutes, until soft and golden brown. Store any leftovers in an airtight container in the refrigerator for up to 3 days.

Acceptable "Junk" Food

It is not unusual for some children with autism to be extremely limited in their food choices. What if fries and other not-so-healthy choices are among the very few options that your child will eat? Try to offer a healthier version of the favored food. For example, roasted potato rounds (or cut into fry shapes) can provide a healthy alternative to French fries. If your child won't try them when first served, try again in the future.

Potato Smashup

You can also leave the skin on the russet potatoes for a different texture in your potatoes. Both russet and new potatoes taste nice with the skin on. Sweet potato skin does not usually taste good in recipes.

MAKES 6 CUPS (6 SERVINGS)

2 sweet potatoes

2 russet potatoes

1½ cups butternut squash

¼ cup butter or coconut oil

½ teaspoon sea salt

½–1 cup milk or nondairy alternative such as unsweetened almond milk

1. Peel potatoes and squash and cube them into pieces of about the same size.

2. Bring pot of water to a boil. Place potatoes and squash in boiling water and boil for about 20 minutes.

3. Drain potatoes and squash and place in mixing bowl.

4. Add butter and salt and smash with a potato masher or hand mixer.

5. Add milk and stir to reach desired texture. Store any leftovers in an airtight container in the refrigerator for up to 3 days.

Roasted Carrots

Careful preparation is needed in this dish to ensure that small children aren't at risk for choking. Roast the carrots so they are soft and easily chewed. Cut the ingredients into pieces that are smaller than the child's windpipe.

MAKES 1½ POUNDS (10 SERVINGS)

8 ounces baby carrots, cut into thirds

1 tablespoon butter, melted

⅛ teaspoon cinnamon

1 tablespoon honey

1 pound red seedless grapes, cut in quarters

1 pear, sliced

1. Preheat oven to 450°F.

2. In the microwave, steam carrots until slightly tender.

3. In separate bowl, melt butter and combine with cinnamon and honey.

4. Remove carrots from microwave. In medium bowl combine all ingredients.

5. Spread out on a baking sheet and roast in preheated oven for 10–15 minutes or until golden and tender. Store any leftovers in an airtight container in the refrigerator for up to 3 days.

Roasting Fruit in the Oven?

Roasting fruits is a wonderful way to bring out their natural sweetness. Winter fruits tend to roast better than summer fruits. Pears, apples, and oranges all roast wonderfully. Lightly toss them with olive oil and a little sea salt and roast them in a 450–500°F oven to caramelize their natural sugars.

Roasted Winter Vegetables

This method works well for any root vegetable, including turnips, rutabagas, and beets.

MAKES 6 CUPS (SERVES 6)

1 large sweet potato

1 small butternut squash

2 medium parsnips

2 tablespoons olive oil

Salt and pepper to taste

1. Preheat oven to 425°F.

2. Peel all vegetables and cut into chunks. (Remove seeds from squash before cutting.)

3. Toss in olive oil and salt and pepper, if using.

4. Spread in a single layer on a cookie sheet.

5. Bake until tender and sweet, approximately 20 minutes. Store any leftovers in an airtight container in the refrigerator for up to 3 days.

Roasted Squash Seeds

If you enjoy roasting pumpkin seeds on Halloween, you will probably enjoy snacking on high-protein roasted squash seeds all year long. Clean the stringy part of the squash off the seeds, spread on a lightly oiled baking sheet, and sprinkle with salt. Bake at 350°F for approximately 15 minutes, watching to ensure that they don't burn. Store in a sealed jar.

Spaghetti Squash with Italian Herbs

Spaghetti squash is also delicious when it is served with a tomato sauce, like the one in the recipe for Shells with Marinara Sauce (Chapter 7).

MAKES 4–6 CUPS

1 spaghetti squash

2 tablespoons olive oil

1 clove garlic, minced

1 teaspoon dried basil

1 teaspoon dried oregano

¼ cup Parmesan cheese or nondairy alternative such as blanched almond flour (optional)

1. Preheat oven to 350°F.

2. Pierce squash with a fork in several places. Bake 1½ hours (1 hour for a small squash).

3. Cut in half and remove seeds. Scrape flesh with the tines of a fork to form spaghetti-type threads.

4. Heat olive oil over medium flame. Add garlic and herbs. Cook 2 minutes or until garlic is golden, but not brown.

5. Toss "spaghetti" with oil and herbs. Top with Parmesan cheese if using. Store any leftovers in an airtight container in the refrigerator for up to 3 days.

Amazing Gluten-Free, All-Natural Spaghetti Squash!

Spaghetti squash works as a pasta stand-in with almost any pasta sauce. Try pestos, tomato-based sauces, or top a serving of spaghetti squash and olive oil with chili.

Sweet Potato Fries

Timesaver tip: Purchase sweet potatoes already peeled and ready to cook! If you use this technique with frozen potatoes, it will help them remain crispy.

MAKES 4 CUPS

4 sweet potatoes, peeled and cut into matchsticks

Large pot of boiling water

Large bowl of ice water

2 egg whites

⅛ teaspoon garlic powder

1. Preheat oven to 450°F.

2. Blanch the sweet potatoes: Bring a large pot of water to a boil. Place sweet potatoes in and cook for 5 minutes. Drain and immediately plunge into bowl of ice water.

3. Dry the sweet potatoes well. Combine egg whites and garlic powder.

4. Toss sweet potatoes with egg white mixture.

5. Line baking sheet with parchment paper and bake for 14 minutes.

6. Turn once about 7 minutes into cooking. Sweet potatoes are done when they are fork tender. Store any leftovers in an airtight container in the refrigerator for up to 3 days.

Why So Many Steps for Sweet Potato Fries?

The moisture content of sweet potatoes is very high and often makes for very soggy fries. The blanching and parchment paper all help to prevent soggy fries. One last tip: Make sure not to crowd the baking sheet with too many potatoes. If they are too close, they steam each other and then become soggy.

Veggie Stuffing

Stuffing isn't just for the holidays! Try this delicious vegetable-based stuffing as a side dish for a weeknight meal. To make bread crumbs, toast 8 pieces of gluten-free bread in a 200°F oven for 10–15 minutes, or until relatively dried out. Chop toasted bread into ½" pieces.

MAKES 6 CUPS

4 tablespoons butter or coconut oil

2 carrots, peeled and coarsely chopped

1 celery stalk, coarsely chopped

1 onion, finely chopped

1 cup chopped button mushrooms

¼ teaspoon freshly ground black pepper

½ teaspoon gluten-free poultry seasoning

4 cups gluten-free bread crumbs

2 cups gluten-free broth (vegetable, chicken, or beef)

1. Preheat oven to 350°F. Grease a 2-quart casserole.

2. Melt butter over a medium flame. Sauté vegetables until soft.

3. Add seasonings, sauté another 2–3 minutes. Add bread crumbs, and toss to mix. Add broth, and toss to mix.

4. Spread mixture in casserole dish and cover with foil. Bake for 35–45 minutes. Remove foil and bake for an additional 10–15 minutes until the top is crispy and golden brown.

5. For a more crisp stuffing/dressing, bake for an additional 15–20 minutes, until stuffing is the consistency you desire. Store any leftovers in an airtight container in the refrigerator for up to 3 days.

Gluten-Free Breads

There are a wide range of breads that are gluten-free available at your local natural foods store. Choices range from brown rice, tapioca, or mixed-grain breads. Experiment with different options to find the ones that you like best. Most of these breads taste best when they are toasted and eaten right away.

Stuffing for Roasted Turkey

Make your own gluten-free cornbread for stuffing a day or two before, cube, and place in the refrigerator in a plastic bag until ready to use.

MAKES ENOUGH STUFFING FOR 1 TURKEY (15 SERVINGS)

1 onion, finely chopped

4 stalks celery with tops, finely chopped

4 tablespoons olive oil

1 pound bulk gluten-free breakfast sausage

10 cups cubed gluten-free or gluten-free cornbread

1 cup gluten-free butter or coconut oil, melted with ½ cup water

2 teaspoons dried thyme

10 fresh sage leaves, minced, or 2 tablespoons dried

2 large tart apples, peeled, cored, and chopped

Salt and pepper to taste

1. In a large frying pan, sauté the onion and celery in the olive oil. Add the sausage and break up with a wooden spoon. Cook until sausage is done and vegetables are tender. Place in a very large bowl.

2. Add the rest of the ingredients to the bowl. Mix the ingredients well by tossing with a spoon.

3. Spread mixture in one or two large greased casserole dishes and cover with foil. Bake for 35–45 minutes. Remove foil and bake for an additional 10–15 minutes until the top is crispy and golden brown.

4. For a more crisp stuffing/dressing, bake for an additional 15–20 minutes, until stuffing is the consistency you desire. Store any leftovers in an airtight container in the refrigerator for up to 3 days.

Vary Your Stuffing

You can make this stuffing really come alive with extra ingredients such as fresh oysters, shucked and chopped; dried cranberries; or coarsely chopped pecans or walnuts.

Pumpkin Risotto

This colorful dish makes a lovely meal when paired with a protein such as beans or meat, and a green salad or green vegetable. It also makes a great addition to a Thanksgiving feast!

MAKES 5 CUPS (10 SERVINGS)

1 tablespoon olive oil

1 tablespoon butter or additional olive oil

1 tablespoon fresh sage

1 clove garlic

¼ cup chopped onion

1 cup Arborio rice

1 cup canned pumpkin

3 cups gluten-free vegetable broth

1. Preheat oven to 350°F.

2. In a small skillet, heat olive oil and butter over medium-high heat.

3. When oil mixture is sizzling, add sage and minced garlic. Sauté 1 minute.

4. Transfer herb mixture to a 3-quart casserole.

5. Add remaining ingredients and cover.

6. Bake 1 hour until most of the liquid has been absorbed by the rice, and the rice is cooked, but still has bite. Stir before serving.

Winter Squash

Pumpkin is a gourd-style squash, similar to acorn squash or butternut squash. They can be interchanged for good results in many recipes.

Mixed Vegetable Kabobs

Serve these kabobs with quinoa, beans, and some sliced melon for a complete summertime meal.

MAKES 2 KABOBS

1 carrot

1 red bell pepper

4 mushrooms

1 small zucchini

1 green bell pepper

2 tablespoons olive oil

Salt and pepper, to taste

1. Peel carrot, and chop all vegetables into 1½" pieces.

2. Toss with olive oil and salt and pepper, if using.

3. Grill or broil for 10–15 minutes on each side, until the vegetables are tender, turning once.

Alternative Pastas

At many well-stocked grocery stores there are a variety of pastas available made from gluten-free grains. These options run the gamut from brown rice to quinoa or corn. Try them with tomato-based sauces, in soups, or tossed with olive oil and pepper and fresh herbs.

CHAPTER 10

DESSERTS

Blueberry Sorbet

This all-fruit sorbet is a great way to provide vitamin C in a fun way.

MAKES 2¼ CUPS (4 SERVINGS)

1½ cups blueberries
½ cup lemonade
2 tablespoons apple juice concentrate

1. Combine all ingredients in a blender or food processor, and purée until smooth.
2. Pour into a freezer-safe container.
3. Freeze for 2 hours, then fluff with a fork.
4. Return to freezer.
5. Continue fluffing every 1½–2 hours until serving.

Broiled Pineapple and Vanilla Frozen Yogurt

This "dessert" provides protein, calcium, and vitamin C.

MAKES 2 CUPS

8 ounces vanilla yogurt or nondairy alternative such as So Delicious Coconut Milk Yogurt
1 cup pineapple chunks

1. Transfer yogurt to a freezer-safe container.
2. Freeze for 1 hour, stir, and return to freezer.
3. Preheat oven to broiler setting.
4. Broil pineapple until slightly browned, approximately 10 minutes.
5. If yogurt is frozen too hard, let sit on counter for a few minutes to soften. Stir in pineapple chunks before serving.

Sweet Potato Pie

This pie has a soft texture because it is egg-free. Make sure to chill the pie for several hours before serving for a more firm texture. Alternatively, if you can tolerate eggs, leave out the ground flaxseeds and water and add 2 eggs to the sweet potato mixture before baking.

SERVES 9
• • • • • • • • • •

1 Basic Pie Crust (see Chapter 2)

2 cups sweet potato purée

½ cup pure maple syrup

½ teaspoon nutmeg

¼ teaspoon ginger

1 teaspoon gluten-free vanilla

2 tablespoons flaxseed meal + 4 tablespoons water OR 2 large eggs

1. Preheat oven to 425°F.

2. Prebake pie crust for 5 minutes.

3. In a medium bowl, combine sweet potato purée, syrup, nutmeg, ginger, and vanilla.

4. In a small bowl, combine flaxseed and water. Let sit 3–4 minutes.

5. Mix flaxseed mixture into sweet potato mixture.

6. Pour filling into pie crust.

7. Bake for 15 minutes.

8. Reduce heat to 350°F, and bake for another 40–45 minutes.

9. Cool completely on the counter before placing in the refrigerator to chill for at least 4 hours before serving.

Apple Pie

Top warm slices of this pie with vanilla ice cream for an all-American treat.

SERVES 9
• • • • • • • • • •

2 gluten-free pie crusts (either store-bought or Basic Pie and Tart Pastry in Chapter 2)

6 Granny Smith apples

1 teaspoon cinnamon

¼ teaspoon allspice

½ cup packed light brown sugar

2 tablespoons arrowroot starch or tapioca flour

1. Preheat oven to 375°F.

2. Prebake 1 crust for 5 minutes.

3. Peel and thinly slice apples.

4. Toss apple slices with cinnamon, allspice, brown sugar, and arrowroot starch.

5. Fill pie crust with apple slices.

6. Top pie with second crust.

7. Pierce top of pie crust with a knife to create steam vents.

8. Bake 40 minutes. Allow pie to cool for at least 30 minutes before slicing and serving.

Vanilla Cake or Cupcakes

These gluten-free, egg-free cupcakes have a light, fluffy texture and pair well with either Chocolate Frosting (see this chapter) or Vanilla Frosting (see this chapter).

MAKES 1 SINGLE-LAYER 8" OR 9" CAKE OR 12 REGULAR CUPCAKES

1 cup brown rice flour

½ cup arrowroot starch or tapioca starch

¾ cup coconut palm sugar or vegan sugar

½ teaspoon xanthan gum

2 teaspoons baking powder

¼ teaspoon baking soda

¼ teaspoon sea salt

¾ cup almond milk

⅓ cup applesauce

¼ cup light-tasting olive oil or canola oil

2 tablespoon gluten-free vanilla extract

1. Preheat the oven to 350°F. Line one 9" round baking pan with parchment paper or a muffin pan with cupcake liners spritzed with nonstick cooking spray.

2. Sift together the brown rice flour, arrowroot starch, coconut palm sugar, xanthan gum, baking powder, baking soda, and salt. Set aside.

3. In another bowl whisk together almond milk, applesauce, oil, and vanilla extract. Mix until well blended. Mix the wet ingredients into the dry ingredients and stir until you have a thick batter. Fold in the chocolate chips, if desired. Pour batter into the greased cake pan or fill cupcake liners ⅔ full.

4. Place on middle rack in preheated oven and bake for 15–18 minutes for cupcakes or 18–25 minutes for a single layer, or until a toothpick inserted into the middle of the cake comes out clean.

5. Remove cake or cupcakes from oven and allow to sit for at least 10 minutes before moving to a wire rack to finish cooling. Cool cake or cupcakes completely before frosting.

Double Chocolate Cake or Cupcakes

Feel free to double this cake for a large 9" x 13" sheet cake or for a large two layer cake. These chocolate, gluten-free, egg-free cupcakes are perfect for a child's birthday party. If your child is not a big fan of frosting, simply serve the cakes dusted with powdered sugar instead.

MAKES 1 SINGLE-LAYER 8" OR 9" CAKE OR 12 REGULAR CUPCAKES

⅓ cup brown rice flour

⅓ cup sorghum flour

⅓ cup arrowroot starch or tapioca starch

½ cup cocoa powder

¾ cup coconut palm sugar or vegan sugar

½ teaspoon xanthan gum

2 teaspoons baking powder

¼ teaspoon baking soda

¼ teaspoon sea salt

¾ cup almond milk

½ cup applesauce

¼ cup light-tasting olive oil or canola oil

1 tablespoon gluten-free vanilla extract

Optional: ⅓ cup mini allergen-free chocolate chips such as Enjoy Life brand

1. Preheat the oven to 350°F. Line one 9" round baking pan with parchment paper or a muffin pan with cupcake liners spritzed with nonstick cooking spray.

2. Sift together the brown rice flour, sorghum flour, arrowroot starch, cocoa powder, coconut palm sugar, xanthan gum, baking powder, baking soda, and salt. Set aside.

3. In another bowl whisk together almond milk, applesauce, oil, and vanilla extract. Mix until well blended. Mix the wet ingredients into the dry ingredients and stir until you have a thick batter. Fold in the chocolate chips, if desired. Pour batter into the greased cake pan or fill cupcake liners ⅔ full.

4. Place on middle rack in preheated oven and bake for 15–18 minutes for cupcakes or 18–25 minutes for a single layer, or until a toothpick inserted into the middle of the cake comes out clean.

5. Remove cake or cupcakes from oven and allow to sit for at least 10 minutes before moving to a wire rack to finish cooling. Cool cake or cupcakes completely before frosting.

Chocolate Frosting

Chocolate frosting is the perfect topping for either Vanilla Cupcakes (see this chapter) or Chocolate Cup-cakes (see this chapter).

**MAKES 2½ CUPS
(FROSTS 12 CUPCAKES)**
....

½ cup Spectrum Palm Shortening,
  softened

½ cup cocoa powder

2 teaspoons gluten-free vanilla extract

2 cups sifted confectioners' sugar (such
  as Wholesome Sweetener's Organic
  brand)

2–3 tablespoons water

With a hand mixer, beat together shortening, cocoa pow-der, vanilla extract, and confectioners' sugar. Slowly add enough water to reach desired consistency. You want the frosting to be stiff enough to hold its shape, but soft enough to easily spread.

Vanilla Frosting

You can add gluten-free food coloring to this vanilla frosting to create multicolored treats.

MAKES 2½ CUPS

2 tablespoons gluten-free shortening

2 tablespoons butter or additional gluten-free shortening

1½ teaspoons gluten-free vanilla

2–3 tablespoons milk or nondairy alternative such as almond milk

2¼ cups powdered sugar

1. In a food processor, combine shortening, butter, vanilla, and 2 tablespoons milk.

2. Add in powdered sugar, and blend until smooth. If the frosting is too thick, add more milk until spreadable.

Cherry Apple Coconut Rice Pudding

Since frozen cherries already have the pits removed, using them dramatically limits the prep time in this dish. You can make this dish a little lighter with light coconut milk if needed.

MAKES 4 CUPS (4 SERVINGS)

1 cup Arborio rice

1 (15-ounce) can coconut milk

1 cup frozen cherries, thawed

1 cup chunky applesauce

1. Preheat oven to 325°F.

2. Rinse rice.

3. Combine all ingredients and place in a covered casserole.

4. Bake 1 hour until the rice has absorbed most of the liquid. Serve warm or chill for several hours.

Best Chocolate Chip Cookies

In any "poll" asking people what their favorite cookie is, the number one result will almost always be the humble chocolate chip cookie. One trick with a perfectly "gooey-on-the-inside-but-crunchy-on-the-outside" chocolate chip cookie is to make sure not to overbake them. Seven to nine minutes is all they need!

SERVES 24

¼ cup Spectrum Palm Shortening

¼ cup white sugar

¾ cup brown sugar

1 egg OR 1 tablespoon ground flaxseeds mixed with 2 tablespoons warm water

1 tablespoon gluten-free vanilla extract

½ cup arrowroot starch

¾ cup sorghum flour

½ teaspoon sea salt

¼ teaspoon xanthan gum

1 teaspoon baking powder

½ teaspoon baking soda

1 cup semisweet chocolate chips

1. Preheat oven to 350°F. Line 2 baking sheets with parchment paper and set aside. In a large bowl cream together shortening, white sugar, and brown sugar. When thoroughly combined, stir in the egg and vanilla.

2. In a smaller bowl whisk together arrowroot starch, sorghum flour, sea salt, xanthan gum, baking powder, and baking soda. Slowly stir dry ingredients into the creamed sugar mixture. Stir chocolate chips into the thick batter.

3. Drop batter 1 teaspoon at a time about 2" apart onto the lined baking sheets. Bake for 7–9 minutes, just until the edges of the cookies are golden brown and the top is just slightly brown.

4. Remove from oven and allow to cool on the baking sheets for 15–20 minutes before removing to a cooling rack.

5. Store cookies in an airtight container on the counter for up to 2 days. These cookies are best the day they are made. They can also be frozen (either as raw dough or as a baked cookie) for up to 2 months.

Sorghum Flour

Sorghum is a cereal grain that has been used as a food source for thousands of years in other parts of the world, especially in developing nations. Sorghum flour is used in this recipe because some people felt that brown rice flour gave the cookies a grainy texture.

Hot Chocolate

Add an ice cube or two to make hot chocolate "not quite so hot" for sensitive mouths. Top with gluten-free marshmallows for a fun wintery treat.

MAKES 1 CUP

1 tablespoon sugar

2 teaspoons cocoa

½ teaspoon gluten-free vanilla

1 cup milk or nondairy alternative such as almond milk

1. In an empty coffee cup, combine sugar, cocoa, and vanilla.

2. In a small saucepan, heat milk until hot, but not boiling.

3. Add milk to chocolate mixture and serve warm.

Where's the Gluten in Vanilla?

Vanilla extract is usually the result of vanilla beans that have been soaked in alcohol. For a vanilla to be gluten-free, it must have been extracted using an alcohol derived from a nonglutinous grain. If a vanilla doesn't say that it's gluten-free, choose another brand or call the company to verify if it's gluten-free.

Lemon Raspberry Ice Pops

Vitamin C takes a refreshing turn in this sweet treat.

MAKES 3 ICE POPS

½ cup lemonade

½ cup raspberry purée

1. Combine lemonade and raspberry purée.
2. Pour into a clean, empty ice cube tray.
3. Cover ice cube tray with aluminum foil or plastic wrap.
4. Poke a craft stick through a slit in each of the filled ice cube spots.
5. Freeze until solid and remove foil or plastic wrap.
6. If it is difficult to get the pops out of the tray, run the bottom of the ice cube tray under warm water to loosen.

Strawberry Kiwi Popsicles

These super-easy, low-sugar popsicles are the perfect summer treat. If you don't have popsicle molds for the freezer simply use small plastic or paper cups. Fill them ⅔ full and place aluminum foil over the top of the cups. In the middle of the foil cut a small hole with a knife and insert wooden popsicle sticks.

MAKES 6 POPSICLES

¼ cup water

3 tablespoons sugar

16 ounces fresh strawberries

2 kiwi, peeled and sliced

1. In a microwave-safe bowl mix together water and sugar. Heat in the microwave for about 60 seconds on high until the sugar has melted into the water to create a simple syrup.

2. Combine simple syrup and strawberries in a blender or food processor; blend until smooth.

3. Place 1–2 slices of kiwi in the sides of each popsicle mold. Then fill the molds ¾ full with the strawberry/syrup mixture.

4. Add tops to popsicle molds and freeze for 4–5 hours before serving.

Mango Honeydew Sorbet

Sweet honeydew and flavorful mango combine for an interesting frozen combination.

SERVES 4

½ medium honeydew
1½ cups mango chunks
½ cup apple juice

1. In a food processor or blender, purée all ingredients together.
2. Pour into a freezer-safe container.
3. After 1½–2 hours, fluff sorbet with a fork, then return to freezer.
4. After 2 hours, fluff sorbet with a fork.
5. Continue fluffing every 2 hours until ready to serve.

Orange Coconut Sorbet

Sweet and creamy, this dessert adds important fat and vitamin C.

MAKES 3 CUPS (3 SERVINGS)

2 cups orange juice

1 cup coconut milk

1. Combine juice and milk.
2. Pour into a covered freezer-safe container.
3. After 1½–2 hours, fluff with a fork, and return to freezer.
4. Continue fluffing every 2 hours until ready to serve.

Softening Sorbet

Sorbet can harden if left in the freezer overnight. Take sorbet out of the freezer and let sit on the counter for 5 minutes to allow it to soften before serving.

Apple Pear Crisp

This fruity dessert is great served with some ice cream on top!

MAKES 4 CUPS (8 SERVINGS)

3 medium pears

3 large apples

¾ cup packed light brown sugar

1 teaspoon gluten-free vanilla

½ cup brown rice flour

¼ cup gluten-free rolled oats

¼ cup melted butter or olive oil

Nonstick cooking spray, or additional olive oil for greasing the pan

1. Preheat oven to 400°F.

2. Peel and thinly slice pears and apples.

3. In a small bowl combine brown sugar, vanilla, brown rice flour, rolled oats, and melted butter. Set aside.

4. Spray a 2-quart casserole with cooking spray.

5. Spread fruit in bottom of casserole.

6. Top with sugar mixture.

7. Bake 40 minutes until golden brown and the fruit is bubbling along the edges.

Pineapple Coconut Rice Pudding

With these three ingredients in the pantry, making this tasty, wholesome dessert is a snap.

MAKES 4 CUPS (8 SERVINGS)

1 (15-ounce) can coconut milk

1 (15-ounce) can crushed pineapple in juice

1 cup Arborio rice

1. Preheat oven to 325°F.

2. In a small saucepan, bring coconut milk and crushed pineapple with juice to a boil.

3. Rinse rice with cold water through a colander.

4. Combine rice with heated coconut milk and pineapple mixture and pour into a 2–3-quart casserole dish. Cover dish with an ovensafe lid or aluminum foil.

5. Bake 1 hour until rice has absorbed most of the liquid, but is still creamy.

Strawberry Cantaloupe Sorbet

Since this frozen treat has no added sugar, it can be served as a healthy snack on a hot day, as well as a dessert.

MAKES 4 CUPS (4 SERVINGS)

½ medium cantaloupe

1½ cups strawberries

½ cup apple juice

1. In a food processor or blender, purée all ingredients together.

2. Pour into a freezer-safe container.

3. After 1½–2 hours, fluff sorbet with a fork, then return to freezer.

4. Every 2 hours, fluff sorbet with a fork.

5. Continue this process until ready to serve.

Pyrex Casserole Dishes Are Not Just for Baking

A covered Pyrex casserole is the ideal container for making sorbet. The shallow rectangle shape makes it easy to store sorbet in a crowded freezer. Furthermore, the easy-to-remove lids keep freezer odors out, while keeping liquid in. An added bonus is that colorful sorbet looks great in a glass container, leading to an impressive display while serving tableside. If Pyrex isn't available, a stainless steel mixing bowl covered with aluminum foil works well, too.

Vanilla Maple Rice Pudding

Serve a scoop of this pudding warmed with some blueberries on the side.

MAKES 4 CUPS (8 SERVINGS)

1 cup Arborio rice

4 cups milk or nondairy alternative such as almond milk

½ cup pure maple syrup

2 tablespoons gluten-free vanilla

1. Preheat oven to 325°F.
2. Rinse rice.
3. In a small saucepan, bring milk, maple syrup, and vanilla to a boil.
4. Combine liquid and rice in a covered 2-quart casserole dish.
5. Bake 1 hour until most of the liquid has been absorbed by the rice and the dish has a creamy pudding-like texture.

Vanilla, the Tropical Flower

Vanilla beans come from a member of the orchid family. They originated in Mexico, but are widely grown throughout the tropics, especially in Madagascar. The beautiful flavor and aroma of the vanilla bean is used in baked goods, confections, and perfumes around the world.

Vanilla Raspberry Sorbet

For a seedless sorbet, press mixture through a fine-mesh sieve before freezing.

MAKES 2¼ CUPS (2 SERVINGS)

2 cups raspberries

1½ teaspoons gluten-free vanilla

3 tablespoons apple juice concentrate

1. Purée all ingredients in a food processor or blender.
2. Pour into a freezer-safe container.
3. Freeze for 2 hours, then fluff with a fork.
4. Return to freezer.
5. Continue fluffing every 1½–2 hours until serving.

Raspberries and Blackberries, a Black Belt in Good Health

Both raspberries and blackberries are rich with antioxidants. Antioxidants are believed to protect your body's cells from damage caused by tobacco, radiation, and even the unhealthy by-products of food you eat.

Chocolate Nut Clusters

There is no reason to go without special-occasion treats when making your own candies is so easy and delicious.

MAKES 16 CANDIES

1 cup chocolate chips

1 cup cashew pieces (or other nut, like pecans or walnuts)

1. Fill a mini muffin pan with muffin papers.

2. Heat chocolate chips over medium-low flame, stirring constantly until almost completely melted.

3. Remove from heat and continue stirring until chocolate is completely melted.

4. Stir nuts into melted chocolate.

5. Use a teaspoon to fill muffin papers.

6. Refrigerate candies for at least 1½ hours before serving.

Chocolate Coconut Brownies

These brownies are a great treat to bring as a potluck dessert. The coconut gives it an excellent flavor and texture!

MAKES 12 BROWNIES

¾ teaspoon light brown sugar

½ cup coconut oil

1½ teaspoons gluten-free vanilla

1 (12-ounce) package chocolate chips

½ cup + 2 tablespoons brown rice flour

½ cup + 2 tablespoons arrowroot starch or tapioca starch

1 tablespoon xanthan gum

½ teaspoon baking soda

½ teaspoon salt

½ cup applesauce

½ teaspoon baking powder

½ cup finely shredded coconut

1. Preheat oven to 350°F.

2. Combine brown sugar and coconut oil in a large microwave-safe bowl. Microwave on high for 1–2 minutes until coconut oil is melted.

3. Stir oil and brown sugar, mix in the vanilla and half the chocolate chips. Set aside.

4. In a medium bowl, combine flour, arrowroot starch, xanthan gum, baking soda, and salt.

5. In a small bowl, combine applesauce and baking powder. Mix applesauce mixture into coconut oil–chocolate mixture.

6. Mix dry ingredients into wet. Stir remaining chocolate chips and shredded coconut into batter.

7. Lightly oil an 8"- or 9"-square pan with coconut oil. Spoon batter into pan. Bake 35 minutes or until a toothpick inserted into the center comes out clean. Cool completely before cutting.

No Microwave? No Problem!

If you don't have a microwave to make these brownies, that's no problem. Heat the coconut oil and brown sugar in a small saucepan, stirring continuously until the coconut oil is melted.

Golden Marshmallow Treats

Get creative with this as a base! Add different nut butters, or experiment with different dried fruits such as dried apricots, strawberries, or even gluten-free chocolate!

MAKES 12 TREATS

8 tablespoons butter or coconut oil

10 ounces gluten-free and vegan Rice Mellow Crème or gluten-free marshmallows

6 cups Rice Chex

¼ cup peanut butter (optional)

½ cup golden raisins

1. Melt the butter in a large skillet over medium-low heat.

2. Add the Rice Mellow Crème and stir frequently until they are melted together.

3. Add the Rice Chex, peanut butter, and raisins.

4. Stir until all of the ingredients are thoroughly coated.

5. Spread the Rice Chex mixture into a greased 9" × 13" casserole dish.

6. Allow to cool. Cut into squares and serve.

Chocolate-Coated Strawberries

Keep these strawberries in the refrigerator until ready to serve; they will start to melt in a warm room.

MAKES 16 STRAWBERRIES

16 fresh strawberries with leaves attached

⅔ cup chocolate chips

1. Wash strawberries, and let them dry completely.

2. In a small saucepan, partially melt chocolate chips over medium heat, stirring constantly.

3. Once halfway melted, remove from heat, and continue stirring until completely melted.

4. Dip strawberries, one at a time, in the melted chocolate.

5. Place coated strawberries on a wax-paper-covered cookie sheet.

6. Refrigerate strawberries for at least ½ hour before serving.

Chocolate Pudding

Although prepared gluten-free puddings are available at the grocery store, it's great to be able to make this creamy treat with ingredients that are often on hand.

MAKES 2½ CUPS (5 SERVINGS)

¼ cup cocoa

¼ cup sugar

1½ teaspoons gluten-free vanilla

¼ cup water, divided

2 tablespoons cornstarch

2 cups milk or nondairy alternative such as almond milk

1. In a small bowl, mix cocoa, sugar, and vanilla. Add hot water, 1 tablespoon at a time until dissolved into a thick paste.

2. In a separate bowl, mix cornstarch and 2 tablespoons cold water until dissolved.

3. Heat milk in a medium saucepan over medium heat.

4. Add chocolate paste and stir until completely dissolved.

5. When chocolate mixture is at a high simmer, just before boiling, add cornstarch mixture, reduce heat, and stir continuously until thickened.

6. Transfer pudding to bowls and refrigerate.

CHAPTER 11

ODDS AND ENDS

Basic Applesauce

Sweeter apples like Golden Delicious will yield a sweeter applesauce, while tarter apples such as Granny Smith will result in an applesauce with a little more kick.

MAKES 2 CUPS
....
2½ cups chopped, peeled apples
½ teaspoon cinnamon, optional

1. Place apple chunks in a large saucepan.
2. Sprinkle on cinnamon if using.
3. Cover apples with water.
4. Bring to a high simmer over medium-high heat.
5. Cook until apples break apart and are very soft. Remove from heat and stir to break up any large chunks. Store in an airtight container in the refrigerator for up to 1 week.

Thick or Thin?
While chunky applesauce can be great as a snack, smooth applesauce is what you should use for baking. To get that great chunky texture, stir the warm applesauce with a wooden spoon just enough to break up the really big chunks. To make smooth applesauce, transfer chunky applesauce to a blender or food processor and blend until smooth.

Baked Tortilla Chips

Experiment with other types of gluten-free tortillas instead of corn for an interesting variation.

MAKES 40 CHIPS (5 SERVINGS)

5 corn tortillas

Canola oil

Sea salt

1. Preheat oven to 350°F.
2. Cut tortillas into 8 wedges each.
3. Spread oil on cookie sheet with a brush.
4. Spread tortilla wedges on cookie sheet in a single layer.
5. Brush tops of tortilla wedges with oil and sprinkle with salt.
6. Bake 13–15 minutes, until golden and crispy.

Some Snacking Ideas

Not every morsel that goes into your child's mouth is likely to be homemade. There are some great snacks that can make being out and about a little easier. Here are some ideas: fruit cups, gluten-free pretzels, rice or corn cereal mixed with raisins, and applesauce cups.

Cinnamon Yogurt Fruit Dip

Children love to dip, and this is a quick and easy yogurt dip that can be used with fruit or with vegetables! Using dips is a great way to increase your children's intake of healthy fruits and vegetables.

MAKES 1 CUP

1 (8-ounce) container vanilla yogurt or nondairy alternative such as So Delicious Coconut Milk Yogurt

2 teaspoons wildflower honey

½ teaspoon cinnamon

1. Combine and stir the ingredients until smooth.

2. Drizzle over fruit or use as a dip.

Cinnamon Is More Than a Good-Tasting Spice
Researchers have shown that ½ teaspoon of cinnamon per day may help to lower blood glucose in people with type 2 diabetes by decreasing insulin resistance. Use cinnamon daily by adding ½ teaspoon to oatmeal or sweet potatoes as part of your family meal plan or by using a cinnamon stick in teas, juice, or even coffee.

Easy Gravy

Dips and sauces can make it easier to tempt picky palates. Use gravies, sauces, and dips to dress up steamed vegetables, broiled meats or tofu, or fruits.

MAKES 1 CUP
....

1 gluten-free bouillon cube (vegetable, chicken, or beef)

1 cup plus 2 tablespoons water

¼ teaspoon poultry seasoning

¼ teaspoon sea salt

¼ teaspoon freshly ground black pepper

1 tablespoon cornstarch

1. Dissolve bouillon cube in 1 cup boiling water.

2. Add poultry seasoning, salt, and pepper to bouillon.

3. In a separate small bowl, thoroughly combine cornstarch with 2 tablespoons cold water.

4. Add diluted cornstarch to other mixture, stirring for several minutes until combined and thickened. Store in an airtight container in the refrigerator for up to 1 week.

Sensory Issues at the Table

Children who are sensitive to texture might be willing to give an otherwise unacceptable food a try if it's served with something appealing. Try serving a wide variety of foods with a favorite sauce or dip. Although ketchup-dipped cantaloupe might not be your cup of tea, it just might get some important nutrients past your child's lips.

Trail Mix

Take along this iron- and protein-rich snack to stave off hunger pangs when on the go.

MAKES 2 CUPS (4 SERVINGS)

½ cup almond slices

½ cup sunflower seeds

½ cup dried cherries

½ cup raisins

3 tablespoons chocolate chips (optional)

Combine all ingredients. Store in an airtight container on the counter for up to 2 weeks.

Hummus

To increase the spiciness of this dish, add one or two cloves of pressed garlic or ¼ teaspoon of cayenne pepper.

MAKES 2 CUPS

2 cups cooked garbanzo beans (homemade or canned)

2 teaspoons lemon juice

2 tablespoons tahini (sesame seed paste)

3 tablespoons olive oil

1 clove garlic

¼ teaspoon cumin

⅛ teaspoon salt

1. If using canned garbanzo beans, drain and rinse beans.

2. Combine all ingredients in a food processor or blender.

3. Process until smooth. Serve as a dip or sandwich spread. Store in an airtight container in the refrigerator for up to 1 week.

Guacamole

Guacamole is a healthy and easy dip that children will love. Use it for dipping raw carrot sticks, celery, green peppers, and tortilla chips.

MAKES 2 CUPS (4 SERVINGS)

2 avocados

2 tablespoons finely chopped sweet onion

1 medium tomato, chopped

2 tablespoons fresh cilantro, chopped

1 tablespoon lime juice

1. Mash avocados with a potato masher or fork.

2. Add remaining ingredients to the mashed avocados. Mix all ingredients together thoroughly. Store in an airtight container in the refrigerator for up to 3 days.

Thank You, Aztec Civilization

It is believed that the higher fat content of the avocado was an important part of the otherwise relatively low-fat Aztec diet. The mash that we know of today is surprisingly similar to what the Aztecs savored in their day.

Hummus Yogurt Dipping Sauce

This yogurt hummus tastes great when served with homemade Baked Tortilla Chips (see this chapter). Or serve with fresh vegetables for dipping.

MAKES 2½ CUPS (5 SERVINGS)

1 (15-ounce) can garbanzo beans

1–2 cloves crushed garlic

1 tablespoon lemon juice

½ cup plus 1 tablespoon plain yogurt or nondairy alternative such as So Delicious Coconut Milk Yogurt

1 teaspoon sea salt

½ teaspoon cumin

1. Drain can of beans and save liquid.

2. In a food processor, combine all ingredients and blend well.

3. Use liquid from garbanzo beans to thin hummus to desired consistency. Store in an airtight container in the refrigerator for up to 1 week.

Pineapple Salsa

Grilled pineapple can make a nice addition to this salsa. Cut a fresh pineapple into ½"-thick slices. Place on medium-hot grill and grill for 5–7 minutes per side. Allow to cool before using in cold salsa dish.

MAKES 4 CUPS (4 SERVINGS)

1 cup diced fresh pineapple

½ cup red pepper, diced

½ cup yellow pepper, diced

½ cup black beans, drained and rinsed

¼ cup red onion, diced

¼ cup cilantro, finely chopped

¼ cup orange-pineapple juice

2 tablespoons lime juice

Salt and pepper to taste

1. In large bowl, combine pineapple, red pepper, yellow pepper, black beans, onion, and cilantro and mix well.

2. In small bowl, combine orange-pineapple juice and lime juice. Pour into large bowl.

3. Mix all ingredients together; season with salt and pepper to taste. Store in an airtight container in the refrigerator for up to 1 week.

Refried Pinto Beans

This is a mild version of a Mexican classic dish. To spice it up, you can add either seeded, chopped fresh jalapeño or canned chopped jalapeño.

MAKES 2 CUPS

1 cup dried pinto beans
 (or 1 [15-ounce] can)
1 tablespoon olive oil
½ onion, finely chopped
1 clove garlic, minced
1 teaspoon cumin

1. If using dried beans, soak 6–8 hours or overnight before cooking.

2. Drain soaking water from beans, rinse, and combine beans with 3–4 cups water. Bring to a simmer with lid tilted.

3. Cook 1–1½ hours or until tender.

4. Drain and rinse either cooked beans or canned beans if using.

5. In a medium saucepan or sauté pan, heat olive oil over medium heat.

6. Add onion and garlic.

7. Cook until onion is tender, 3–5 minutes.

8. Add beans and cumin and heat through.

9. Remove from heat and mash with a potato masher or fork. Store in an airtight container in the refrigerator for up to 1 week.

Creamy Salsa Dip

This dip makes snack time fiesta time. Serve with Baked Tortilla Chips (see this chapter) or veggie slices. It also makes a nice base for a Mexican-style wrap sandwich.

MAKES 2 TABLESPOONS

1 tablespoon mayonnaise

1 tablespoon mild salsa

½ teaspoon honey

1. Combine all ingredients.

2. Stir thoroughly. Store in an airtight container in the refrigerator for up to 1 week.

Sweet Sunflower-Seed Butter Dip

Serve this sweet dipping sauce with cold steamed broccoli florets, baby carrots, or apple slices.

MAKES 2 TABLESPOONS (OR 1 SERVING)

1 tablespoon vanilla yogurt or nondairy alternative such as So Delicious Coconut Milk Yogurt

1 tablespoon sunflower-seed butter

1 teaspoon honey

1. Combine all ingredients in a small bowl.

2. Stir well and serve.

Tropical Pudding Pie Dip

This tropical dip is a hit with kids! Serve this dip with an arrangement of in-season fruit to help your children try fruits that have not been tried before!

MAKES 3 CUPS (3 SERVINGS)

1 small package gluten-free instant vanilla pudding

1½ cups milk or nondairy alternative such as almond milk

1 cup vanilla yogurt or nondairy alternative such as So Delicious Coconut Milk Yogurt

⅓ cup orange-pineapple juice

½ teaspoon orange or lemon zest

1. Combine vanilla pudding and milk with a beater.

2. Once blended well, add remaining ingredients and blend until smooth.

3. Chill and serve. Store in an airtight container in the refrigerator for up to 1 week.

Sweet Potato Spread

Serve this sweet spread to add vitamins to a slice of gluten-free toast or crackers.

MAKES 1 CUP

1 cup grated raw sweet potato

¾ cup water

1 teaspoon pure maple syrup

¼ teaspoon cinnamon

⅛ teaspoon nutmeg

2 tablespoons applesauce

1. Bring sweet potato and water to a boil and keep boiling for 5 minutes.

2. Reduce heat to low and stir in remaining ingredients. Store in an airtight container in the refrigerator for up to 1 week.

Yogurt Applesauce Dip

This dip works well for all kinds of fruit. It is easy to make in small batches or in large batches for family meals or gatherings.

MAKES 2 TABLESPOONS, OR 1 SERVING

1 tablespoon applesauce

1 tablespoon vanilla yogurt or nondairy alternative such as So Delicious Coconut Milk Yogurt

¼ teaspoon cinnamon

1. In a small bowl, combine all ingredients with a spoon.

2. Stir well and serve.

Homestyle Gravy

This is a great basic gravy recipe that you can use to ladle over meats, chicken, and potatoes and other veggies. Substitute beef broth for chicken broth if you're serving the gravy with beef.

SERVES 12
....

½ teaspoon olive oil

½ cup chopped onion

1 teaspoon dried thyme

1½ tablespoons cornstarch

¼ cup water

1¼ cups gluten-free chicken broth

¼ teaspoon salt

¼ teaspoon pepper

¼ teaspoon poultry seasoning

1. Coat a medium saucepan with olive oil and heat over medium-high heat. Add onion and dried thyme. Sauté until onion is tender, about 3 minutes.

2. Combine cornstarch and water in a small jar with a screw top. Shake until smooth and there are no lumps. Set aside.

3. Add broth to saucepan. Slowly stir in cornstarch mixture, stirring until smooth and well blended.

4. Add salt, pepper, and poultry seasoning to onion mixture. Bring to a boil, stirring constantly. Continue stirring and cooking until bubbly and thickened. Store in an airtight container in the refrigerator for up to 1 week.

Avocado Yogurt Dip

This sweet and creamy dip can also be used as a dressing for a green salad.

MAKES 1 CUP

½ ripe avocado

¼ cup plain yogurt or nondairy alternative such as So Delicious Coconut Milk Yogurt

1 teaspoon honey

2 tablespoons orange juice

1. Mash avocado with fork or potato masher.

2. Add remaining ingredients.

3. Stir until smooth. Store in an airtight container in the refrigerator for up to 1 week.

Fresh Croutons

These can be made in advance and stored in the refrigerator, then crisped up at the last moment. Double the recipe for extras.

**MAKES 24 CROUTONS
(4 SERVINGS)**

¼ cup olive oil

2 cloves garlic, minced or put through a garlic press

4 slices gluten-free bread, thickly cut, crusts removed

Salt and pepper to taste

1. Preheat the broiler to 350°F.

2. Mix the oil and garlic. Brush both sides of the bread with the garlic oil. Sprinkle with salt and pepper to taste.

3. Cut each slice of bread into 6 cubes to make 24 cubes. Spray a cookie sheet with olive oil. Place the cubes on the sheet and broil until well browned on both sides.

4. Put the cookie sheet on the bottom rack of the oven. Turn off the oven and leave the croutons to dry for 20 minutes.

5. Store in an airtight container for up to 2 weeks until ready to use.

For the Love of Garlic

Garlic will give you various degrees of potency depending on how you cut it. Finely minced garlic, or that which has been put through a press, will be the strongest. When garlic is sliced, it is less strong, and when you leave the cloves whole, they are even milder.

ONLINE GLUTEN-FREE RESOURCES FOR PARENTS

RESOURCE	WHERE TO FIND IT
Gluten-Free Support Groups	*http://bit.ly/11aDq69*
National Foundation for Celiac Awareness	*http://bit.ly/5ozGRg*
Books for Gluten-Free Kids	*http://bit.ly/14s42DT*
Gluten-Free 101, All the Basics	*http://bit.ly/120gDzT*
GFree Kid: a website for GF kids and parents	*http://gfreekid.com/*
Celiac and Gluten-Free Bloggers with free recipes, tips, etc.	*http://bit.ly/peY2hy*
Cheryl Harris: a gluten-free registered dietitian and nutritionist	*www.harriswholehealth.com*
Gluten-Free Kids Central from Celiac Central	*http://bit.ly/ox6Kfh*

STANDARD U.S./METRIC MEASUREMENT CONVERSIONS

VOLUME CONVERSIONS

U.S. Volume Measure	Metric Equivalent
⅛ teaspoon	0.5 milliliter
¼ teaspoon	1 milliliter
½ teaspoon	2 milliliters
1 teaspoon	5 milliliters
½ tablespoon	7 milliliters
1 tablespoon (3 teaspoons)	15 milliliters
2 tablespoons (1 fluid ounce)	30 milliliters
¼ cup (4 tablespoons)	60 milliliters
⅓ cup	90 milliliters
½ cup (4 fluid ounces)	125 milliliters
⅔ cup	160 milliliters
¾ cup (6 fluid ounces)	180 milliliters
1 cup (16 tablespoons)	250 milliliters
1 pint (2 cups)	500 milliliters
1 quart (4 cups)	1 liter (about)

WEIGHT CONVERSIONS

U.S. Weight Measure	Metric Equivalent
½ ounce	15 grams
1 ounce	30 grams
2 ounces	60 grams
3 ounces	85 grams
¼ pound (4 ounces)	115 grams
½ pound (8 ounces)	225 grams
¾ pound (12 ounces)	340 grams
1 pound (16 ounces)	454 grams

OVEN TEMPERATURE CONVERSIONS

Degrees Fahrenheit	Degrees Celsius
200 degrees F	95 degrees C
250 degrees F	120 degrees C
275 degrees F	135 degrees C
300 degrees F	150 degrees C
325 degrees F	160 degrees C
350 degrees F	180 degrees C
375 degrees F	190 degrees C
400 degrees F	205 degrees C
425 degrees F	220 degrees C
450 degrees F	230 degrees C

BAKING PAN SIZES

U.S.	Metric
8 × 1½ inch round baking pan	20 × 4 cm cake tin
9 × 1½ inch round baking pan	23 × 3.5 cm cake tin
11 × 7 × 1½ inch baking pan	28 × 18 × 4 cm baking tin
13 × 9 × 2 inch baking pan	30 × 20 × 5 cm baking tin
2 quart rectangular baking dish	30 × 20 × 3 cm baking tin
15 × 10 × 2 inch baking pan	30 × 25 × 2 cm baking tin (Swiss roll tin)
9 inch pie plate	22 × 4 or 23 × 4 cm pie plate
7 or 8 inch springform pan	18 or 20 cm springform or loose bottom cake tin
9 × 5 × 3 inch loaf pan	23 × 13 × 7 cm or 2 lb narrow loaf or pâté tin
1½ quart casserole	1.5 liter casserole
2 quart casserole	2 liter casserole

INDEX